THE PENG

Poetry of the Con

POETRY OF THE COMMITTED INDIVIDUAL

A *Stand* Anthology of Poetry

*Edited with
an introduction by
Jon Silkin*

PENGUIN BOOKS
in association with Victor Gollancz

Penguin Books Ltd, Harmondsworth, Middlesex, England
Penguin Books Inc., 7110 Ambassador Road, Baltimore, Maryland 21207, U.S.A.
Penguin Books Australia Ltd, Ringwood, Victoria, Australia

—

First published by Victor Gollancz in hardback, and
by Penguin Books in paperback, 1973

—

Made and printed in Great Britain by
Cox & Wyman Ltd, London, Reading and Fakenham
Set in Monotype Bembo

CONTENTS

CONTENTS

CONTENTS

CONTENTS

The translator's name appears at the end of the relevant poem or group of poems.

ACKNOWLEDGEMENTS

For permission to reprint the poems in this anthology acknowledgement is made to the following:

For DANNIE ABSE: 'The Water Diviner', 'Hunt the Thimble' from *Selected Poems*, to Hutchinson Publishing Group.

For DAVID AVIDAN: 'Kas Buvo – Tai Nebus', to ACUM and to the author/translator.

For JOHN BARRELL: 'Some Versions of Pastoral', to the author.

For WENDELL BERRY: 'The Sorrel Filly' from *Farming: A Hand Book*; reprinted by permission of Harcourt Brace Jovanovich, Inc.

For JOHN BERRYMAN: 'The Search' from *Love and Fame*, to Faber & Faber.

For ALEXANDER BLOK: 'The Twelve', to the translator, Alex Miller.

For JOHANNES BOBROWSKI: 'The Duna', to the translators, Ruth and Matthew Mead. English translation copyright 1964 Matthew Mead.

For BERTOLT BRECHT: 'And he did not compare', 'E. P. L'Élection de son Sépulchre', 'Of All Works', to Methuen & Co. Ltd, and to the translator, Michael Hamburger.

For T. J. BRINDLEY: 'Joan's Essay', to the author.

For JOSEPH BRODSKY: 'The Jewish Cemetery near Leningrad', to the translator, Daniel Weissbort.

For ALAN BROWNJOHN: 'A Teacher of the Deaf' from *The Railings*, to Digby Press.

For LEON FELIPE CAMINO: 'And for what have I come?', to the translator, Peter Glusker.

For ANTONIO CISNEROS: 'From a Mother again', 'Loneliness II', 'On the Death of the Bishop, who was truly of Your Ilk', 'Paracas' from *Peru: The New Poetry*, to London Magazine Editions and to the translator, David Tipton.

For PETER DALE: 'Unposted Letter', to the author.

For GUNNAR EKELÖF: 'Xoanon', from *Gunnar Ekelöf: Selected Poems* (Penguin Modern European Poets), to the translators, W. H. Auden and Leif Sjöberg; 'A world in each human being', to the translator, Ann Draycon, 'Byzantium' and 'Someone said: I saw a dancing man', to the translator David McDuff.

For HANS MAGNUS ENZENSBERGER: 'Karl Heinrich Marx' from *Poems*, to Martin Secker & Warburg Ltd, and to the translator, Michael Hamburger.

For ROY FISHER: 'For Realism', 'Seven attempted Moves', 'Continuity', 'Five Morning Poems from a Picture by Manet', 'The Making of the Book' from *Collected Poems 1968* and *Matrix*, to Fulcrum Press.

For PAAVO HAAVIKKO: 'The fir-trees at play', 'One thing at a time' from *Selected Poems*, to Cape Goliard, and to the translator, Anselm Hollo.

For JOHN HAINES: 'It must all be done over', 'The Goshawk', 'The Middle Ages', 'The Wreck', from *The Stone Harp*, to André Deutsch.

For MICHAEL HAMBURGER: 'Arctic Explorer', 'Homage to the Weather', 'Tides', 'Mad Lover, Dead Lady', 'Psychosis' from *Weather and Season*, to Longmans, Green & Co., and to the author.

For TONY HARRISON: 'The Nuptial Torches' from *The Loiners*, to London Magazine Editions.

For JOHN HAYNES: 'Stickman', to the author.

For JOHN HEATH-STUBBS: 'Watching Tennis', 'Titus and Berenice', 'A Few Strokes on the Sand' from *Selected Poems*, to Oxford University Press, to David Higham Associates, Ltd and to the author.

For ZBIGNIEW HERBERT: 'A Parable about Russian Émigrés', 'The Captain's Spy-glass', to the translator, Adam Czerniawski. Copyright Adam Czerniawski.

For NAZIM HIKMET: 'Letters to Taranta Babu' from *Selected Poems*, to Jonathan Cape Ltd and to the translator, Taner Baybars; 'Sunday', to the translator, Iain White.

For GEOFFREY HILL: 'A Song from Armenia', 'Funeral Music', 'Locust Songs', 'September Song', 'The Assisi Fragments' from *King Log*, to André Deutsch Ltd.

For ANSELM HOLLO: 'Empress Hotel Poems' from *Maya*, to Cape Goliard.

For MIROSLAV HOLUB: 'Discovery of Fire', 'Oxidation' from *Although*, to Jonathan Cape Ltd and to the translators, Ian and Jarmila Milner, and 'The Heart', 'A Nazi Air-Raid Warden', 'School', to the translator, George Theiner.

For PETER HUCHEL: 'The Journey', 'Under the Constellation of Hercules', to the translator, Henry Beissel. Copyright Henry Beissel.

For PHILIP LEVINE: 'They feed they Lion', 'A Soldier of the Republic', to Kayak and to the author.

For EMANUEL LITVINOFF: 'To T. S. Eliot', to the author.

For GEORGE MACBETH: 'Cranach's Hunts', to the author.

For SORLEY MACLEAN: 'Poems II, XXVII, XXXII, XXXVII, LII' from *Poems to Eimhir*, to Victor Gollancz Ltd, Northern House, and to the translator, Iain Crichton Smith.

For BARRY MACSWEENEY: 'We sit for Weeks', to the author.

For CHRISTOPHER MIDDLETON: 'Gaunt Man Striding' from *Nonsequences*, to Longmans, Green & Co. and to the author.

For EWART MILNE: 'The Whitman Grasses', to the author.

For NORMAN NICHOLSON: 'Black Guillemot', 'The Elvers', to the author.

For TOM PICKARD: 'The Devil's Destroying Angel' from *The Order of Chance*, to Fulcrum Press.

For MAILA PYLKKONEN: 'The Flowers', to the translator, Anselm Hollo.

For MIKLÓS RADNÓTI: 'Red Shore', 'Roots' from *Cloudy Sky* to Harper & Row, Inc. and to the translators, Steven Polgar, Stephen Berg, S. J. Marks.

For TOM RAWORTH: 'Going to the Zoo' from *Nicht Wahr, Rosie*, to Fulcrum Press.

For TADEUSZ RÓŻEWICZ: 'Draft for a Contemporary Love-Poem', to Rapp and Whiting and to the translator, Adam Czerniawski.

For PENTTI SAARIKOSKI: 'Making The Sun Run', 'Poem' (from 'Greek Sequence'), 'The Madman's Horse' from *Poems*, to Rapp and Whiting and to the translator, Anselm Hollo.

For JON SILKIN: 'A Word about Freedom and Identity in Tel-Aviv', 'Divisions', 'Flatfish', 'Spade', 'Worm', from *Amana Grass* and *Killhope Wheel*, to Chatto & Windus and Midnag.

For IAIN CRICHTON SMITH: 'He said, we argue', 'The Green washed over Them', 'The Politicians Gesture', 'Those who are needed', 'You lived in Glasgow', 'You told me once', to the author.

For KEN SMITH: 'Family Group', 'The Pity', 'Leaving', 'The Night Boat', 'Eli's Poem' from *The Pity* to Jonathan Cape Ltd, to Swallow Press and to the author.

For VLADIMIR SOLOUKHIN: 'Berry', 'The Willow', to the translator, Daniel Weissbort.

For WILLIAM STAFFORD: 'Quaker Meeting', 'The Stranger', to the author.

For MARINA TSVETAYEVA: 'Insomnia 6 & 7', 'Homesickness', 'An Attempt at Jealousy' from *Selected Poems*, to Oxford University Press and to the translator, Elaine Feinstein.

For GIUSEPPE UNGARETTI: 'Agony', 'Another Night', 'Brothers', 'Quiet', 'Stars', 'Vigil', to the translators, Jonathan Griffin and Charles Tomlinson.

For CÉSAR VALLEJO: *Trilce*, nos. lvi, lvii, lx, to the widow, and to the translators, Ed Dorn and Gordon Brotherston.

For ANDREI VOZNESENSKY: 'Earth', 'Goya', 'Parabolic Ballad', 'The first Ice' to the translator, Edwin Morgan.

For JEFFREY WAINWRIGHT: '1815', to the author.

For TED WALKER: 'Cuckoo-pint', 'Grebe', 'Terrains Vagues' from *Fox on a Barn Door*, to Jonathan Cape Ltd.

For NATHAN WHITING: from 'Poems of an ownerless Slave' out of *From while courting the Sergeant's Daughter*, to Pym-Randall Press.

For JAMES WRIGHT: 'The Poor Washed up by Chicago Winter' from *Shall we gather at the River*, to Rapp and Whiting.

For YEVGENY YEVTUSHENKO: 'Stalin's Heirs', to the translator, Edwin Morgan.

For NATAN ZACH: 'A Song for the Wise Lovers', 'Against Parting', 'Giant', 'Honi', 'How is it that one star' to Northern House, to the author and to the translator, Jon Silkin.

INTRODUCTION

Stand is called 'a quarterly magazine of the arts', but for its first three issues it published only poetry. The gradual inclusion of fiction, criticism, and the other arts represents not so much a shift from this original preoccupation with poetry, but a sharing of the available space with other forms. It does not represent even a fractional diminution of concern with poetry but an evident adding to it.

Stand was begun in 1952, when the first phases of neo-romantic poetry had lost much of their enthusiasm and credibility, and when the second phase, although it probably did not know it, was soon to be undermined, but not destroyed entirely, by the composite rationalism of *New Lines*:

> If one had briefly to distinguish this poetry of the fifties from its predecessors, I believe that the most important general point would be that it submits to no great systems of theoretical constructs nor agglomerations of unconscious commands ... One might ... say that George Orwell with his principle of real, rather than ideological, honesty, exerted, even though indirectly, one of the major influences on modern poetry ... The most glaring fault ... when the new period opened was the omission of the necessary intellectual component from poetry.[1]

Much acrimony passed between those adhering to *New Lines* and the *Mavericks*, some sense of whose position is outlined in:

> I suppose I am equating the romantic with the Dionysian and the Dionysian with that mysterious, permanent element in poetry that irradiates and moves us and endures ... But if, for this reason, I am anti-movement, I'm certainly not opposed to discipline and form and style. For these qualities make these disturbing Dionysian elements acceptable to oneself and to others.[2]

1. *New Lines*, ed. Robert Conquest (London 1957), pp. xiv–xvi.
2. *Mavericks*, ed. Howard Sergeant and Dannie Abse (London 1957), p. 10.

The weight of the cutting edge, what drove the blade in the dispute, was that two parties were struggling for ascendancy at a time when it was accepted that only one set of aesthetics could properly exist, and that such received criteria were, for that matter, to provide the continuing basis of a lasting autonomy. This sentimental tyranny is not any longer thought necessary (it may return), and the removal of fashionable constrictions, or at least of an autonomous set of them, has in almost every way been productive. But the loss entailed may be partly measured in the amount of bad poetry now produced by reputable publishers, just as the gain may be counted in the variety, difference, and even existence, of a number of good poets. The present Geoffrey Hill might just have been read in the late fifties, but would the present Roy Fisher, and Tom Pickard as he is here represented?

This change, in which no set of criteria may now be said to dominate, permits the *variety* of good poetry; and whatever may be said about the amount of bad poetry, given the comparative rigidity of English society and its culture, at a time when a revaluation of Britain's position threatens to harden and shrink our responses, we have to accept, gratefully I think, such relative openness. The term for some is euphemistic; they would say that what passes for openness constitutes an evacuation of standards, the result of which is a barbaric lack of concern. Even if this (for me) unacceptable argument were true, we cannot return to the singular rule the argument seems to wish back on us; were we to try, we would produce a repressive situation.

The existence of many different kinds of poets, between whom there is some uneasy rapport, suggests that the 'system' we may have in future may be one in which the criteria will increasingly emerge from the practice of the writers, and not from the imposition upon them of worn-through absolutes. That is, the so-called criteria will be the product of the writers and their work in relation to what they write about; the relations will originate criteria. This is not a covert plea for the discarding of what has been learnt already, but for the open adaptation of it by the writers themselves. What follows from this is not a slippery optimism but some sense of how we are making things new, reconstituting the way in which poets are read, and the relations between them, their readers and critics.

The change I'm considering may be seen in the degree of self-consciousness developed in the poets themselves. It operates among them not only as they recognize and perhaps tolerate the differences between themselves, but as they accept the validities of cultures (and individuals as part of them) that are in most ways different from themselves. The force with which American poetry, in successive waves, has impacted itself on poets in England is a commonplace. And few would question that American poetry, whether it has permanently or temporarily influenced the outward practice of English poetry, has forced it (its readers and poets) into recognizing that it is now sharing the language on different points of a lengthening spectrum, the extension of which is no longer within the sole dictation of England. Such cultural shock as we accommodate to this (and to other situations created by other English-speaking cultures) is in the meantime useful, provided we neither arrogantly refuse to recognize the value of these others, or, conversely, abandon what we have. All we can do, but the movement is a large deliberate one, is to re-examine what we have in relation to these others, and develop it in mutual interaction.

The other way in which the 'outside' has been felt has been through the intermediation of translated work. Islanded, we have usually been in ambiguous relation with other cultures, one moment eagerly taking from them, but then, like a sated infant, thrusting them off. Sometimes this rejection is part of a re-forming and consolidating movement, but it also seems to emerge from uneasiness, or fear:

> There are discreditable reasons, too [as to why translation is 'so popular'] ... In *Akros* recently, D. M. Black took a bleak look at modern English poetry and said the most hopeful sign was the new interest shown by English poets in foreign poetry. This is at the

opposite pole from Larkin's famous dismissal of poetry from abroad ... [but Larkin] got the emphasis right. The poet's true concern is with his own language and the poems he makes from it, not with international good will. He's likely to be no more honest about that than the politician is. I should like to see people interested and knowledgeable about poetry in at least four European languages, but it should be *in* these languages, not in English versions of variable degrees of loyalty to the original. Too many translators (and I include myself) are ill-acquainted with the tongues they translate from and know very little about the prosody and traditions of other languages. You can achieve useful results from this ignorance but that is not what translation is supposed to be about.[3]

Porter does not refer however to the results of the reading of translated poetry – on the reader or the poet. And surely as we now revalue our position, between ourselves and between other cultures and communities, the recognition of these others, through translation, may impinge with especial usefulness. Such awareness is more likely to be obtained in a valuable way through the reading of poetry and fiction, at whatever remove, than through the shifting impressions of journalism. Surely what we need to do is, with as little anxiety as possible, listen to other cultures as they are transposed into our language and respond to them. And I use *respond* advisedly, wanting to suggest with its use that a closer more intimate sense of co-existence may be got through having the poems in our language, notwithstanding that some readers may be able to follow the work in the original. By getting to understand something of perhaps very different cultures, it may help us not to preserve but freely to practise our own, and destroy that possible society of common market cliché and inter-state rule, with each government co-opting the other into fanatical repression of its 'subjects'. The quicker and more thoroughly we learn, in however limited a way, something of what the sensuous powers and moral entrapments feel like in Iowa, Teesside,

3. Peter Porter, *Opinion*, *The Review*, ed. Ian Hamilton (London, no. 22, June 1970).

or Prague (quite apart that is from what Amman, Jaffa and Hanoi can tell us) the more insistently can our preparations be made for a continuingly vigorous and changing culture.

In some ways this last is an indirect reply to the question as to what use poetry is. It's not a question I want to answer here directly, but I have to say, with George Steiner, that I question whether art can have claimed for it its civilizing attribute, while at the same time the holocaust, Stalin's purges, and the Vietnam war, to name three of this century's perhaps comparable barbarisms, occurred within the same era. What kind of connection exists between the 'due appreciation' of art, and barbarism? The word 'appreciation' begs a number of questions that Steiner seems in fact unwilling to develop; for just as we cannot assume that the concentration camp officer wasn't reading Rilke 'well', we may also question whether he was reading 'properly'. There is no way of knowing. There is only the parallel and endlessly disturbing coexistence of cruelty, which is worse than barbarism, with art. Steiner puts this question:

> Because we are trained to give psychological and moral credence to the imaginary, to the character in a play or a novel, to the condition of spirit we gather from a poem, we may find it more difficult to identify with the real world, to take the world of actual experience to heart – 'to heart' is a suggestive phrase. *The capacity for imaginative reflex, for moral risk in any human being* is not limitless [my italics]; on the contrary, it can be rapidly absorbed by fictions, and thus the cry in the poem may come to sound louder, more urgent, more real than the cry in the street outside.[4]

Under this possibility, the heart wilts. Because if nothing is left that will inform and erase our cruelty, what can we look forward to but a decline in which the flesh is melted, and charred into a blackness so omnipresent, the act of cruelty so intense and yet ordinarily and banally present, that we shall be glad to die, and where collective suicide will seem the only *conceivable* virtue. The heart wilts for other reasons. For if part of why we

4. George Steiner, *Language and Silence* (Harmondsworth 1969), pp. 83–4.

write is to fulfil a mimetic urge, where art dramatizes the complexity of impulse, decision and action, if it *will* express itself, there is surely another part which desires to make communicative this expressiveness. And among the bundle of motives, including vanity, that reach through this expressiveness out to another human being, is perhaps the sense of how cruelty may at least be modified, productiveness become a social and shared thing – of how writing can learn, teach and move to action, or at least modify those human actions which at present threaten us with extinction. I cannot reply directly to Steiner's question, partly because I believe the question to contain irrefutable elements. I can only add to it the sense I have of how I, and people I know, have occasionally been shamed and made to feel they must change certain modes of behaviour as a result of being moved, emotionally and intellectually, by something they have read. This is a very slight response to Steiner's question, but I don't think that he raises it in such a way as to dismiss any evidence which might even begin to qualify his inquiry. And if my response is inadequate to the point of being misleading, one might add that perhaps society would be even more cruel were it not for these minimal restraints and exempla that art has made. The point of the question seems to me not by way of doing down art but of bringing it into a central position and, through the teaching of it, communicating its alert possibilities for constructiveness.

All this is crucial to what we have, as co-editors of *Stand*, been trying to do. But the heart suffers diminution because, faced with the gigantic forces of cruelty outside art as well as inside the makers of it, and faced too with the knowledge of impure motives, it is as much as one dares to make even the smallest poem without in some way feeling presumptuous. Faced also with the possibility that art is either useless (ineffectual) or else corrupting in the sense that it uses up (according to Steiner) an unmeasured but certainly limited amount of moral courage and response, one can see, selfishly enough, that society is not only tolerant in allowing us to write at all, but kind enough to indulge us in a self-deception whereby we arrogate to ourselves the notion that we are sensitizing some (few) human beings, ourselves perhaps included. And behind our despair perhaps at this possibility lies, again, the vanity which would assert that creativeness, which is possibly only the dramatization of surplus psychic force that would otherwise turn its possessor mad were it not used – that this creativeness is of use to others; whereas its use is only a means of taming and making socially safe the possessor of such surplus.

I believe that these are not possibilities but probably part-truths. That is, that the element of ego involved in making anything is inseparable from the making, and that it requires a certain hard and controlled humility to recognize this. But once recognized it ceases to be as important as one might at first suppose. The indecencies of creation, among which is the child-like wish to be entirely pure, give way to that movement of communication in which, while the emotion is not robbed of its essentiality, its movement towards another human being acquires, in this intention, some shaping generosity. This is I know absolutely debatable, and one has heard many times how the writer or maker as he or she works (I except perhaps the playwright) is not only not thinking, but cannot think of, his or her audience. Yet we are not living in an era of grunts and shrieks assembled (to reverse Geoffrey Hill's proposition)[5] into a grim florid music, and we are neither naïve nor innocent. And I find it hard to believe that, as we are making the thing, however essential to ourselves it may need to be, that we do not somewhere in us respond to the sense that this is to be shared, and communicated to another. Moreover it seems to me as sentimental to suppose that this is only for motives of vanity as it is to be attributed purely to altruistic impulses. The mind in heat does not hesitate on such fine distinctions – if it does, it loses impetus.

The question of personal (or even private) essentiality as against social communicativeness and usefulness is one that has

5. See below, p. 92.

dogged us as we tried to choose the poems for the magazine, therefore moving it in this or that direction. This sounds too cold. And too calculated, although it might be near the truth. Near, but not near enough, for the fact is that the magazine is not an abstract notion, but the sum of decisions made, an increasing or diminishing but hopefully developing sum, since it is made not only by policies but by available contributions. This is a two-way process, and clearly, where a writer sees in existence a platform for his work that he had not known of, and which if it did not exist would disable (he feels) his work from being published, he will surely feel encouraged to write. And I mean not merely to write, but to follow more essentially what he has to say, where what he has to say is inseparably a part of how he says it. A nuance, a cadence, is an idea. It is so, but perhaps, we may sometimes feel, not sufficiently so. This may be because the nuance is not sufficiently itself, but more often it is surely because the transforming imagination has sieved too little, too little of importance to us.

But this returns me to the question I'd begun to form. In *Agenda* (an issue of which was devoted to Ungaretti) there is a passage from *The Mecs* (12 September 1931), translated by Marielina Freeth:

> It's not less dark [in the desert] when the rays begin to slant – only dazzlingly different. A mask of shadows rises from a broken point in a steep slope. Whoever has witnessed the extremely cautious advance of any one of these shadows, won't find the adjective that it suggests to me strange: thieving shadow. It seems to adhere to nothing, depend on nothing, is thoroughly detached – a lover of paradox might well call it: free shadow. And here I'll have to repeat what has been said by so many painters of the early nineteenth century who were themselves but vainly trying to portray such effects. If I stare at that shadow, little by little it concentrates, it becomes the very nucleus of a picture, surrounded by great fringes of teeming light; and if I keep staring, it takes on the vitreous and metallic transparence of stagnant water. But glittering from an inner dryness, all worn and burnt out like limestone or cinder, this is a water without humidity, a cruel water – not

water that, however infected, however putrid, can quench thirst:
it's a sadistic trick of the light.[6]

This is compelling: the way in which the shadow by being concentrated on finally attracts to itself the attribute of water, the opposite of its context and *substantially* different from itself. Not precisely opposite however, since the water itself is seen to have an inner dryness, worn-through and burnt, as rock and cinder is, and as being something like shadow, like the shadow, perhaps, of what causes its shadow by obstructing light. This containing of one thing in its opposite (see Rosenberg's 'Midsummer Frost') is dramatic, terse, and strong. But it could be effectively argued that this writing has little to do with political realities, and as much with any programme of social usefulness or melioration. It communicates in an extraordinary and supple way (despite its complication) but it precludes any sociality. It shares, but what it shares is not social, unless we may extend the word to include the moving of the mind in an abstraction so fine that it scoops out its 'matter' not even from tactilely experienced substances, but from observed substances and denied ones (shadow). One may argue that extending the mind is socially useful, but to deploy such an argument is already I think to have compromised the main point, which is that this writing gets nowhere near socially committed art.

The question raises the issue in all its apparent absoluteness. The passage dramatizes insight and perception. It implies an exclusion of social questions because the nature of the insight is that it may be perceived only through intense and (probably separate) concentration, only subsequently to be communicated. Moreover, although the passage does not violate the medium of words if only because, as Ungaretti indicates, many painters (of a particular kind) have been unable to visualize the perceptions he has been able to verbalize, the re-application of such insights as the passage has might require very specialized

6. *Agenda*, ed. William Cookson & Peter Dale (London) vol. 8, no. 2, Spring 1970, pp. 78–9.

circumstances. The passage has a kind of diaristic quality which even raises questions as to whether it was, in its initial creation, even conceived for publication. (Eliot would perhaps have argued that communication with oneself, on the level of intense and formulated perception, was enough.) But the decision to publish, on the part either of the writer or the publisher, again engages the question. And it is two-edged in that it is arguable that if this is art, then the propagandistic, the heuristic or didactic art, is not; and vice-versa. Arguable, but not I think tenable. Nor do I believe the dispute is fruitful or necessary: the antinomy is artificial. The real question, for writers, and for us as editors, was how, for instance, these two could be fruitfully combined. Or put in more specific terms, how might a hermetic or imagistic art be engaged with an art that wanted without compromising its essentiality to be socially orientated, involving, as this does, some move towards the discursive.

Ungaretti managed to combine the hermetic with a social awareness in those early poems which seem the *direct* issue of his experiences on the Isonzo front in the First World War.[7] Yet, quite early on in *his* creative life, Herbert Read found objections to the Imagism he had been deeply influenced by. He published these in *Art and Letters* in 1918, and reprinted them again in *The Contrary Experience* (1963). He says, after reproducing his 'definitions towards a Modern Theory of Poetry':

> I admitted that [the Imagists] were the only modern school of poets which showed 'any clarity of creative intention', but I criticized them because 'in their manifestoes they had renounced the decorative word, but their sea-violets and wild hyacinths tend to become as decorative as the beryls and jades of Oscar Wilde.' I also accused them of lacking 'that aesthetic selection which is the artist's most peculiar duty ... We must shrink from the exotic and the decadent' ... This essay must have been written early in 1918 ... before the end of the war ... I think it reflects something of the contradiction that was being forced on us by our daily experience.

7. See below, p. 171.

We were trying to maintain an abstract aesthetic ideal in the midst of terrorful and inhuman events.[8]

The last sentence does I think express the (for him at least) inadequacies of Imagism as a vehicle for his experiences and evaluations. It shows for instance the difficulties of the Imagist poet the moment he wants to write a poem in which some scene-setting, narrative, and multiplication of character, personality or psychology occur. The hard, cold image seems to preclude such concerns.

I don't have any answers; all I can do is to frame the questions, knowing at the same time that Imagism has provided lasting and essential insights for the making of poetry. Essential but partial ones. So that, in varying degrees, many of the problems of what and how we chose for *Stand* came into difficult contact with this problem.

The problem of the hard clear image, and the adjacent implication that the essentiality of the poet's impulse must not be violated, bear on us in our relations with our readership. In selling the magazine in several different ways (in pubs and in colleges and universities, as well as in bookshops and through subscription) how could we hope to make accessible such an intense and self-consciously preoccupied art in a meaningful way? Wasn't this poetry already difficult enough for those who read poetry constantly? What is the 'meaning' of Tom Raworth's 'Going to the Zoo'?[9] Roy Fisher's 'Matrix'[10] also presented difficulties of this kind, and most of the poems we chose were exacting in their various ways. Yet it is at the extremities of one's theories and ideas that one is tested. For even with the more accessible, partially paraphrasable poems, one is aware that paraphrase is only a partial if important means of understanding or explication. That mimetic and dramatic re-enactment of impulse (unparaphrasable) was essential to the poetry we were looking for. Finally could we hope that people

8. Herbert Read, *The Contrary Experience* (London 1963), pp. 175–6.

9. See below, p. 112.

10. *Stand* (Newcastle-on-Tyne), vol. 12, no. 1, Winter 1970–71, pp. 28–31.

would have the patience and willingness to be taxed intellectually and morally with, say, Ken Smith's 'The Pity'?[11] Shortly, yes.

It may be expedient to give that answer, but I think we realized fairly early on that it is presumptuous to offer work provided we believe it is within a reader's compass. What if, for instance, we had read the work and had ourselves been developed and extended by it? Or had read the work and felt (as we did in one instance) that it was beyond our present abilities to account for? H. R. Hays has translated Brecht's fine poem 'Coal for Mike'.[12] It is intelligible on first reading, but it exacts from the reader an assent that is painful as well as inspiriting. It prompts feelings of remission. Could we ask the reader to sit with such a poem (had we published it, that is) with the implication of the reader being asked to work out his or her relationship with what the poem was asking for? Yes to that also. Although I should add that this did not mean we were naïvely unaware of how some readers might reject part of the magazine, reading perhaps the fiction and only some of the poetry. Or both the poetry and the fiction, but perhaps not the criticism.

I should identify some of the work that has for us represented exempla, work that we have been looking for, as well as work that has extended our consciousness of what could be done within a particular area of commitment. Taner Baybars' translation of Hikmet's 'Letters to Taranta-Babu',[13] with its extraordinary co-ordination of explicit attack on Mussolini's onslaught on Ethiopia with a sensuous apprehension of what this entailed, is one instance. The work shows what fascism involved, and apprehends what was being or about to be destroyed. Yet however valuable the sensuous re-creations are, the explicit element is integral. For instance, the last letter of the poem is in

11. See below, pp. 113–14.

12. Bertolt Brecht, *Selected Poems*, trans. H. R. Hays (New York 1959), pp. 106–7.

13. See below, pp. 188–202.

prose, 'it consists [writes Baybars] of statistics which Hikmet must assiduously have put together in order to demonstrate under what conditions the Italians were, at that time, fighting a war against the Abyssinians'. It is not merely that the explicit, intentional element provides the structure from which the sensuous imagery can best strike feelingly through to the reader's senses. It is a crucial and qualifying part of what he has to say. That is, not only is such substance explicitly part of Hikmet's commitments; it additionally acts as some kind of check, or other consciousness, deployed on to the purely sensuous poet (and reader) who might otherwise be content to 'bathe and float' the senses (Arnold's phrase[14]). The relations between the explicit and the sensuous or enacting impulses bear on the problem I was discussing – Imagism and discursiveness, and how these may be brought together. It is problematic, because the nature of Imagism is that it rejects discursiveness; it wants enactment rather than description. And it wants enactment of a kind that also I think tends to reject narrative. So that the question for us has been whether a poem could use the hard, clear and sensuous image in such a way as to share its nature with the explicitly expressed issues without losing its essentiality. In coming to terms with this recalcitrant problem Hikmet borrows back something from the novel; there are characters and relationships in the poem which infuse into the explicit terms, while authorizing the sensuousness, a certain bias from which we cannot as easily escape had the concerns been flatly stated. (Something of the same methods are used by Hikmet in *The Moscow Symphony*, also translated by Taner Baybars.[15]) These elements are used not so much to provide narrative continuity (though something of that is present) but to enable emphases to interact and re-emerge. As Baybars summarizes the poem's 'prolegomenon': 'an Italian friend

14. Matthew Arnold, *Culture & Anarchy*, ed. J. Dover Wilson (London 1961), p. 170. (Although I do not use Arnold's arguments.)

15. Nazim Hikmet, *The Moscow Symphony*, trans. Taner Baybars (London 1970).

writes to Hikmet that he has discovered in a room in one of the poorer districts of Rome, letters written by an Ethiopian negro to his wife in Galla, Ethiopia. The letters had not, of course, been posted, the police having arrested the negro.'

The question of narrative is one which Imagism has, almost by implication, cut from its vocabulary. Pound uses *fragments* of it in the earlier Cantos, and Eliot uses fragmented continuities in *The Waste Land*. But this is really like using narrative as though it were an image. Thus despite Blok's use of fragmentary allusiveness in 'The Twelve',[16] what makes his poem so different from both Pound's and Eliot's is the sense of how the march of the twelve men (and their leader) acts as a cohering element. It both sets the context and provides continuity; indeed the narrative continuity is also part of the symbolic meaning of the poem – the development of the revolution. And because there is such a structure, Blok can integrate into it his criticism of conduct and motivation; of what the revolution liberates which is both productive and destructive. Consider, as the only substantial instance of this latter, section six, which is the culmination of a sub-narrative strand involving one of the marchers in relation to the lovers Katie and Johnny.[17] In 'Loneliness II', Cisneros sustains the poem on episodic narrative and, within this, makes such 'actions' and conversations assess the value and motivation of commitments as they emerge in the poem.

As a rule we do not find this capacity in English poetry. Herbert Read, whose poem 'The End of a War' Yeats 'substituted' for all other war poems,[18] experienced this difficulty of trying to merge narrative structure with Imagism. 'The Happy Warrior' contrives to bring the two together, but the poem is a special instance, and relies in any case for its deepest reading on its being co-ordinated with Wordsworth's 'The Character of

16. See below, pp. 204–15.
17. See below, pp. 178–9.
18. *The Oxford Book of Modern Verse 1892–1935*, ed. W. B. Yeats (London 1936), p. xxxiv.

the Happy Warrior'.[19] Wordsworth's poem is of course discursive. In the longer poems that comprise Read's *Naked Warriors* (1919),[20] narrative structure is used, but the imagistic elements in the poems are diluted in such a way as to enervate them. Read had relied on the imagistic elements to render intensity and expressiveness; the collision of these two modes produced a compromise that harmed both. By the time Read came to write 'The End of a War'[21] (published in 1933) he had worked out a solution: he pushed the narrative outside the poem, setting the scene and describing the events of the episode in a prefacing prose argument which, though essential to the reading of the poem, is in ambiguous relationship to it, and without any relationship to it structurally. It is not integral to the structure in the way that, for instance, Hikmet's last 'letter' is to the whole of his poem. Nevertheless this exclusion allows Read to concentrate more fully on what he wants to do; the poem is reflective, and explores the impulses of nationalism, spiritual pride, and an undirected if genuine humility. The point is easily graspable; Read was in an uneasy relationship with Imagism his whole life. Having criticized it in 1918, and having in his perhaps most ambitious poem come to terms with it without in fact, writing an imagist work, he asserts in *What is a Poem?*

> This new poetic awareness was for a short time called Imagism, and as such was accused of triviality and incoherence . . . I believe that the poets I have mentioned (all of them connected with Imagism, and some of them remaining rigidly within its terms) have written the only certainly perdurable poems in our century, and that poets like W. B. Yeats in his later work and even Robert Frost in his best work were influenced by their example. But I have no wish to be partisan on this occasion.[22]

Geoffrey Hill is clearly a poet having little in common with Read, but he has, I think, similar problems engaging him. With

19. Herbert Read, *Collected Poems* (London 1966), p. 35.
20. op. cit., pp. 29–44.
21. op. cit., pp. 99–113.
22. op. cit., p. 274.

his early 'Genesis'[23] the poem is held together *partly* by using days of the week as a means of tabulating impulsions in sequence. There are other groupings: creation, the emerging of the predatory, the choice of an earth-bound 'blood's pain' over the notion of spiritual rebirth, and the ambivalent recognition of the shedding of blood as in mysterious contingent relationship with man's onwardness. Yet the sequence of days is important to the poem structurally, and through it Hill tries to initiate the image of a growing consciousness, although it is only a proper sequence as it refers back to God's six days of work. The poem itself does not have narrative coherence. The result (lacking genuine narrative) is stylization of a kind that Hill subsequently abandoned. With 'Funeral music',[24] the prose note that precedes the poem stands in similar elucidatory relation to it as Read's 'Argument' does to 'The End of a War', though less close perhaps (or perhaps less close in Hill's mind), for whereas when the poem was first published in *Stand* the note did in fact directly precede the poem, in subsequent publication as part of *King Log*, the note becomes an 'essay' placed at the end of the book. In it he writes:

> Admittedly, the sequence [of poems] avoids shaping characters and events into any overt narrative or dramatic structure. The whole inference, though, has value if it gives a key to the ornate and heartless music punctuated by mutterings, blasphemies and cries for help.
>
> There is a distant fury of battle. Without attempting factual detail, I had in mind the Battle of Towton fought on Palm Sunday, 1461. It is now customary to play down the violence of the Wars of the Roses . . . In the accounts of the contemporary chroniclers it was a holocaust.[25]

The prefatory note scoops together the historical references, and in its own terms brings together some of the material for (prior) consideration and setting. The poems do not form a narrative sequence, although they do lead through the battle

23. Geoffrey Hill, *For the Unfallen* (London 1959), pp. 15–17. But in fact the poem is dated in the text 1952.

24. See below, pp. 89–94.

25. Geoffrey Hill, *King Log* (London 1968), pp. 67–8.

into some (deliberately) incomplete attempt at evaluating the cost in both physical and spiritual excoriation. Evaluation is made partly by reference to a supposed, or possibly supposed, after-life, in which the ideals of an exemplary spiritual life would if anywhere be found; partly by reference to this, or to eternity, yet into which no sense of human evaluation can be extended with the certainty of finding corroborative echoes:

> If it is without
> Consequence when we vaunt and suffer, or
> If it is not, all echoes are the same
> In such eternity. Then tell me, love,
> How that should comfort us – [26]

Even supposed *notions* of an after-life, with its spiritual absolutes, are insufficient here since the first of the unrhymed sonnets opens in platonic supposition; that is, the platonic structure throws into ambiguity the question of whether we are to suppose an after-life is to be believed in; it does this by supplanting the idea of an after-life with its own metaphysical scheme. But in all this, the point I am trying to make about Hill's longer poems or sequences is that where some kind of extended work demands a correspondingly developed structure, Hill meets this problem (at least in 'Funeral music') partly by placing outside the poem those explanations, scene-settings and minimal narrative gestures which would, in his own mind apparently, reduce his concentration of intensity, rhetoric and imagistic impulse. There is no discursiveness, no explanatory matter, no narrative, inside the poetry. The purity of the poetry must remain unimpaired. Even the preceding epigraph to 'September song'[27] ('born 19.6.32 – deported 24.9.42') fulfils a similarly narrative frame. To go further would at this point be to begin saying much more of what the poems are 'about'; what I'm here trying to suggest is that in much English poetry

26. See below, p. 92.
27. See below, p. 95.

subsequent to Imagism narrative and the image are often at odds with each other, and that this is not a helpful situation. There is perhaps an insufficient movement from the unfolding of psychological re-enactment to its re-enactment in the 'world of action'.

That's a poor phrase, bringing to mind not merely the heap of 'events' in an adventure story, but the almost as ludicrous image of a life consisting only of well-ordered simple and continuous causal sequences. But the phrase will have to do since, in its philistinism, it catches on to something of the weakness in much of the best contemporary English poetry. I don't think I should ever want either to publish or write narrative poems; but the tendency to dramatize the psychology of human beings at the expense of showing what actions this psychology entails is, I think, a preference that may finally shrink even the internal world as the poet (and the novelist) conceives it. I mean that it might be profitable at this stage to use and not be used by Imagism, which is strongly, perhaps almost logically, drawn to the dramatization of the inner world.

With Roy Fisher's work the sense of dramatizing mimesis *and* its relations with the outer world is stronger than with Geoffrey Hill. Perhaps 'Five morning poems from a picture by Manet'[28] doesn't adequately show this, since the outer figurative reality is at two removes, coming first (in order of the poet's creation) through the picture and then the poem. The same applies perhaps to Voznesensky's 'Goya',[29] the reference being to Goya's *The Disasters of War*. With Voznesensky the movement back to life, to historical fact, the referential movement, is strong and didactic; but what is interesting here is the nature of Voznesensky's use of Goya. The interpositionary character of Goya's work here does two things. Firstly, it draws on an earlier disaster of war (man's making). Like Christopher Logue's quotation of Brecht's 'When men march off to war' inserted in his translation of Book XVI of Homer's

28. See below, pp. 72–7.
29. See below, p. 223.

Iliad,[30] the Goya 'quotation' reminds us that there is an (ironic) tradition of man's brutality to man. The Russian experience stands in direct but not immediate succession to the Spanish. Such quotation however also reminds us that there is, mercifully, some creative consciousness that will record and evaluate this. Voznesensky is in line with Goya, as Brecht would seem to be with aspects of Homer. But in Voznesensky's poem, the incorporation of Goya's work (in a poem of such small size) seems to mediate between the bestial facts of war and the poet's responses to them. It is as though Voznesensky felt the need in some way to complicate the realism. As though he felt that the direct reproduction of these facts would not be sufficiently evaluative, or make a poem that would have an autonomous life of its own, springing into action the moment it was read. And it's this presence of another 'voice' through which Voznesensky speaks, which sets going these evaluations (in echoing perspective) and gives a greater depth and life to the poem than it might otherwise have. Voznesensky infiltrates Goya's voice with his own, making present within his evaluations earlier corroboration.

It is interesting that although the movement towards figurative reality is not so strong with Fisher in the 'Morning poems' as it is with Voznesensky, the reliance on Manet's work as the interpositionary visual artefact is less. I believe this is so because, as I've suggested, Fisher's poem is more *embryonically* a return to figurative reality than Voznesensky's, and more poised within a visual dramatization of responses. The visual picture is used in the poem as a counterfeit physical reality within which certain responses are interpolated, and it is this that in its turn is used to confront actual reality – both the external and the internal ones of the reader.

In 'Seven attempted moves'[31] (and some contrast can be indicated here) there is a definite move to invest reality with the

30. Christopher Logue, *Patrocleia*; book xvi of Homer's *Iliad*, a translation, (Norfolk 1962).

31. See below, pp. 69–71.

literally static nature of a photograph, and this is to do with what the poem is about. Reality is seen, at first, as discrete particles of imagery, clear, unavoidable, empirical, leading nowhere. It is such a wall of visual data that the reader is made to collide with and experience, in order that he may recognize that, in *fact*, the terror is hovering just beneath these images. As though society offered this set of well-ordered images (post-Auschwitz, but then, again, not too well-ordered) against which the naive or uncomprehending or deliberately obtuse citizen must come, not seeing, since society does not wish him to see, the actual reality, the terrible destruction of human beings. In the poem the wall or sheet of images is flecked, sometimes streaked, with the events they seek to hide; what in fact Fisher does is to create a picture which is neither a picture of secretive human activity nor a picture of what is being concealed, but an ominous and guilty image of both – since, as he suggests, what we have to experience is both. The act of hiding creates for us the sense of terror, since we can only wish to hide what, in such a context, is terrifying. The nature of the confrontation with Fisher's 'picture' is fearful; it is also unlike what we might experience, or would be meant to experience, if we were merely to confront the outward semblances, or else the picture of semblances that has been manufactured for us by 'the State'. The picture Fisher composes is interpretative. Chairs are frightening, not because of what they are (seen as), but for what they have been made to do:

> Here are the schoolroom chairs on which
> the ministers, in the playground,
> Sat to be shot

(almost, one might say, 'sat to be photographed' – the word 'sat' is here very nearly a pun)

> Four chairs; the property
> Of the Department of Education ...[32]

Yet even in such a fine assemblage as 'Seven attempted

32. ibid.

moves', the method is discontinuous, if mergingly cumulative. There are no actual figures, only the remains, the sediments of persons. But, as Fisher might indicate, this is as it should be; it is in fact what the State wishes. Only the traces of people may be permitted; no actual persons or groups of people with continuous lives are (unfortunately) possible.

The interesting thing is that we've published in many instances the kind of poetry that only partly comes to terms with the problems as I've been outlining them. But I have to add that such partial coming to terms seems, in its context, absolutely relevant to the quality of life we have. The experience of concentration camps, and totalitarianism, has been diffused throughout consciousness and we have lost what little innocence we might have possessed. We can only return to life, fully to life, gradually if at all. This must sound gratuitously ungrateful, but what I'm trying to suggest is that, firstly, these are my biases, and that, secondly, the nature of these poets' achievements is not only important, but, in some ways at least, astonishing. The western poet finds difficulty in speaking of the holocaust, for instance, but this is not surprising since it is out of his very civilization that this has emerged; yet it is out of such 'civilization', for and with it, that he has to speak.

A last point. It is generally assumed that the way in which a committed poet has to speak if he is to be effective, and retain his humanity, is to dramatize sensuously his concerns, fleshing them with human substance and responsiveness. Ideas do not in the abstract make poems. And to give them substance, we must use images. Yet there is at least surely one poet who does not demonstrate this. Michael Hamburger quotes in his *The Truth of Poetry* his translation of Brecht's poem on the workers' uprising in East Berlin:

'The Solution' ('Die Lösung')

After the uprising on June 17th
The Secretary of the Authors' Union
Had leaflets distributed in the Stalinallee
Which said that the people

Had forfeited the government's confidence
And could only win it back
By redoubled labour. Wouldn't it
Be simpler in that case if the government
Dissolved the people and
Elected another?[33]

There are no metaphoric images in the poem, and, for that matter, no visually reproductive ones; it is an instance of how committed writing can be effective as poetry without being fleshed in imagery.

The image has come under the suspicions of a few poets, Hill amongst them. In a poem, first published in *Preghiere*, he notes

I am circumspect,
Lifting the spicy lid of my tact
To sniff at the myrrh.
('Three Baroque Meditations'; no. 2)[34]

The image, it might be said, is too often confection fed to a glutted and pampered consumer; it achieves nothing beyond its sensory and local pleasures. Consciousness is not extended. Hamburger's poem on Eichmann, 'In a Cold Season',[35] with similar austerity implies the same kind of point. One might add that Hamburger's poems, by the persistence of their tone and rhythm, as well as by their refusal to stretch the image into making more than deceptively simple and naturalistic visualization, create proportions that resist any imaginative excess; that is, they are exemplary.

These are I suppose provisional statements. But it's worth adding that I have never wanted to publish poems that were almost instantly disposable. If we write partly to compete with our mortality, and if the society in which we live makes that mortality even more precarious, that is a further reason for our trying to make something that isn't for immediate disposal.

33. Michael Hamburger, *The Truth of Poetry*, (London 1969), p. 188.
34. Geoffrey Hill, *King Log*, (London 1968), p. 47.
35. Michael Hamburger, *Weather and Season*, (London 1963), pp. 27–31.

But perhaps, periodically, we are bound to experience what amounts to loss of nerve. It's this that needs watching.

Stand is produced communally, and it is our hope that a sense of collaboration emerges from this anthology. This aspect needs emphasizing; with many magazines one has the sense (perhaps wrongly) that many of the names on the editorial board are editorially non-functional. In the main we do not, however, operate a majority rule, or rather we do not set this down as the only way in which decisions are taken. If one person feels strongly that this poem or that story should not be included, then the strength of his or her feelings is the operative factor in the decision. All the poems in this anthology have been published in *Stand*. Where the poet or the translator has subsequently revised the text of any poem we have used the new version if he wished us to do so, hence the differences (in a few cases) between what was first printed and what appears here.

Stand has been edited by, in various combinations, Ken Smith, Catherine Lamb, Gene Baro, Jon Silkin, Lorna Tracy and John Byrne; Tony Harrison edited it for a year, and during that time produced the Czechoslovakian issue. Ed Brunner and Howard Fink are editors for the U.S.A. and Canada respectively. Michael Wilding is the Australian editor.

The growth of the magazine is in many ways attributable to the Northern Arts Association, who in 1965 invited me to move north to Newcastle-on-Tyne and combine *Stand* with the *North East Arts Review*, then being published by the Association. Since then Northern Arts has given generous financial assistance to the magazine, and that support is acknowledged here as it is in each issue of *Stand*.

JON SILKIN
58 Queens Road,
Newcastle-on-Tyne,
July 1971

EWART MILNE

The Whitman grasses

It is pleasant to stare at animals
They are as a rule well-shaped creatures
Their skin ripples and has no lesions:

It is pleasant to work with animals
They are as a rule well-educated creatures
Especially donkeys and muscular farm horses

But to live with animals is not to live like animals:
True, many a man would be a swan to surprise Leda sleeping
Or a bull to carry off some delectable Madam Europa

Also some of our forefathers were forced to live like geese
Cropping the roadside grasses to stay the pangs of their bellies:
But to be impelled by desire or circumstance into the animals' world

Is not to live happily or at peace in their kingdom.
America, America, what have they done to thee?
That noble savage who lived with nature, where is he?

It is pleasant and instructive to stare at animals
But it is neither pleasant nor instructive to live as animals
In a jungle of bricks-and-mortar tooth-and-claw all our own.

SORLEY MACLEAN

(from *Dain do Eimhir, Poems to Eimhir*)

2.

And if our language says that love
and reason are the same
she's lying.

When first your beauty struck my eyes
they did not learn to be wise,
they weren't scholars of such terms.

When first I heard your voice, my clay
was not sundered in this way,
not the first time.

The assault was more indirect
against my heart and intellect.
Later, the storm grew strong.

With all I had of prudence
I fought in my defence.
I used sagacious eloquence.

And from my ancient wisdom I
spoke from the chaos of the sky:
'I do not want you here nor yet away.'

My love was on the inside,
my wisdom remained outside,
that thin partition was destroyed.

And reason spoke to my love thus:
'How foolish is this doubleness.
Love is the reason we possess.'

27.

The reader told me my imagination
was gathering to a conflagration,
lustrous, brilliant and clear,
But, dearest, it was your face
that fashioned this astounding grace,
you are the origin of the force
and abundant constancies of my verse.

32.

Let me lop from my verse every grace
shed by the lustre of your face,
and let it learn the economy
of Liebknecht's death and slavery:
let me burn away each leaf
that grew joyfully from my grief.
And let me hammer the people's wrongs
into the iron of my songs.

37.

It was not your body's beauty,
or the beauty of your brilliant face,
blaze of that blinding bandage
that dazzled my hurt eyes,
but the impeccable spirit's beauty
that moved within my haunted gaze,
the clear beauty of your spirit.
That was the marrow of my praise.

52.

To my scrutiny you were a star
shining in the sky's roof
and you were given the two lights
of my fertile spirit and my grief.

And therefore you blazed with three,
in one trinity, fire-bright.
But these, my vehement lights, were only
echoes of your own light.

I waited for the power that would
disfigure your virtue in its course:
but I offered you the three together
at the end of ten years.

Though if it were my own two lights
that gave such splendid power to yours
surely their brightness would be quenched
by brutal time in ten years.

O cheerfulness and open heart
ablaze in a clear virtuous face:
deceit of heart, deceit of eyes
so imaged in your lustrous grace.

Surely not long was that pursuit
though it was ten years and more –
when a chance sight of beauty brought
the hope an eternity could desire.

(*Iain Crichton Smith*)

NORMAN NICHOLSON

The elvers

An iron pipe
Syphoning gallons of brine
From the hundred foot below sea-level mine –
A spring salty as mussels,
Bilberry-stained with ore;
And the pink, dry-paper thrift rustles
In the draught made by the spray
As the pumps thrust the water upward
To a rock-locked bay.

And, quick in the brown burn,
Black whips that flick and shake,
Live darning-needles with big-eye heads –
Five-inch elvers
That for twice five seasons snake
Through the earth's turn and return of water
To seep with the swell into rifts of the old workings
And be churned out here on cinder beds and fern.

The pumps pour on;
The elvers shimmy in the weed. And I,
Beneath my parochial complement of sky,
Plot their way
From Sargasso Sea to Cumberland,
From tide to pit,
Knowing the why of it
No more than they.

The black guillemot

Midway between Fleswick and St Bees North Head,
The sun in the west,
All Galloway adrift on the horizon;
The sandstone red
As dogwood; sea-pink, sea-campion and the sea itself
Flowering in clefts of the cliff –
And down on one shelf,
Dozen on dozen pressed side by side together,
White breast by breast,
Beaks to the rock and tails to the fish-stocked sea,
The guillemots rest

Restlessly. Now and then,
One shifts, clicks free of the cliff,
Wings whirling like an electric fan –
Silhouette dark from above, with under-belly gleaming
White as it banks at the turn –
Dives, scoops, skims the water,
Then, with all Cumberland to go at, homes
To the packed slum again,
The rock iced with droppings.

I swing my binoculars into the veer of the wind,
Sight, now, fifty yards from shore,
That rarer auk: all black,
But for two white patches where the wings join the back,
Alone like an off-course migrant
(Not a bird of his kind
Nesting to the south of him in England),
Yet self-subsistent as an Eskimo,
Taking the huff if so much as a feather
Let on his pool and blow-hole
In the floating pack-ice of gulls.

But, turn the page of the weather,
Let the moon haul up the tide and the pressure-hose of spray
Swill down the lighthouse lantern – then,

When boats keep warm in harbours and bird-watchers in bed,
When the tumble-home of the North Head's rusty hull
Takes the full heave of the storm,
The hundred white and the one black flock
Back to the same rock.

EMANUEL LITVINOFF

To T. S. Eliot

Eminence becomes you. Now when the rock is struck
your young sardonic voice which broke on beauty
floats amid incense and speaks oracles
as though a god
utters from Russell Square and condescends,
high in the solemn cathedral of the air,
his holy octaves to a million radios.

I am not one accepted in your parish,
Bleistein is my relative and I share
the protozoic slime of Shylock, a page
in Sturmer, and, underneath the cities,
a billet somewhat lower than the rats.
Blood in the sewers. Pieces of our flesh
float with the ordure on the Vistula.
You had a sermon but it was not this.

It would seem, then, yours is a voice
remote, singing another river
and the gilded wreck of princes only
for Time's ruin. It is hard to kneel
when knees are stiff.

But London Semite Russian Pale, you will say
Heaven is not in our voices.
The accent, I confess, is merely human,
speaking of passion with a small letter
and, crying widow, mourning not the Church
but a woman staring the sexless sea
for no ship's return,
and no fruit singing in the orchards.

Yet walking with Cohen when the sun exploded
and darkness choked our nostrils,
and the smoke drifting over Treblinka

reeked of the smouldering ashes of children,
I thought what an angry poem
you would have made of it, given the pity.

But your eye is a telescope
scanning the circuit of stars
for Good-Good and Evil Absolute,
and, at luncheon, turns fastidiously from fleshy
noses to contemplation of the knife
twisting among the entrails of spaghetti.

So shall I say it is not eminence chills
but the snigger from behind the covers of history?
Let your words
tread lightly on this earth of Europe
lest my people's bones protest.

JOHN HEATH-STUBBS

Watching tennis

Light, in light breezes and a favouring sun,
You moved, like a dancer, to the glancing ball,
And the dance and the game seemed one
To me, unmarked spectator by the wall –

Always spectator – in-apt at any sport –
And you free burgess of the summer air:
Embraced within the Iron Maiden, Thought,
I of my body's poverty am aware.

How could I guess that all-consoling night,
Confider and concealer of secrets, should conduct
You home to port within my clumsy arms?

Yet, by the chances of the game betrayed,
Your mouth on mine made known its silent need,
And all my sense found peace among your limbs.

Titus and Berenice

'Turn to me in the darkness,
  Asia with your cool
Gardens beyond the desert,
  Your clear, frog-haunted pool;
I seek your reassurance –
  Forget, as I would forget,
Your holy city cast down, the Temple
  That still I desecrate.'
'Buzz!' said the blue-fly in his head.

'In darkness master me,
  Rome with your seven hills,

Roads, rhetorical aqueducts,
  And ravaging eagles;
Worlds are at bitter odds, yet we
  Have found our love at least –
Not expedient to the Senate,
  Abominable to the priest.'
'Buzz!' said the blue-fly in his head.

Titus the clement Emperor
  And she of Herod's house
Slobbered and clawed each other
  Like creatures of the stews;
Lay together, then lay apart
  And knew they had not subdued –
She the insect in his brain,
  Nor he her angry God.

Note: According to a Jewish tradition Titus was afflicted with an insect in his brain as a punishment for his destruction of the Temple.

A few strokes on the sand

Old men, as they grow older, grow the more garrulous,
Drivelling *tempores acta* into their beards,
Argumentative, theoretical, diffuse.

With the poet, not so. One learns
To be spare of words; to make cold thrusts
Into the frosty air that comes.

The final message – a few strokes on the sand;
A bird's footprints running to take off
Into the adverse wind.

DANNIE ABSE

Hunt the thimble

Hush now. You cannot describe it.

Is it like heavy rain falling,
and lights going on, across the fields,
in the new housing estate?

Cold, cold. Too domestic, too
temperate, too devoid of history.

Is it like a dark windowed street at night,
the houses uncurtained, the street deserted?

Colder. You are getting colder,
and too romantic, too dream-like.
You cannot describe it.

The brooding darkness then,
that breeds inside a cathedral
of a provincial town in Spain?

In Spain, also, but not Spanish.
In England, if you like, but not English.
It remains, even when obscure, perpetually.
Aged, but ageless, you cannot describe it.
No, you are cold, altogether too cold.
Aha – the blue sky over Ampourias,
the blue sky over Lancashire for that matter . . .

You cannot describe it.

. . . obscured by clouds?
I must know what you mean.

Hush, hush.

Like those old men in hospital dying,
who, unaware strangers stand around their bed,
stare obscurely, for a long moment,

at one of their own hands raised –
which perhaps is bigger than the moon again –
and then, drowsy, wandering, shout out, 'Mama!'
Is it like that? Or hours after that even:
the darkness inside a dead man's mouth?

No, no, I have told you:
you are cold, and you cannot describe it.

The water diviner

Late, I have come to a parched land
doubting my gift, if gift I have,
the inspiration of water
spilt, swallowed in the sand.

To hear once more water trickle,
to stand in a stretch of silence
the divine pen twisting in the hand:
sign of depths alluvial.

Water owns no permanent shape,
brags, is most itself in chaos;
now, under the shadow of the idol,
dry mouth and dry landscape.

No rain falls with a refreshing sound
to settle tubular in a well,
elliptical in a bowl. No grape
lusciously moulds it round.

Clouds have no constant resemblance
to anything, blown by a hot wind,
flying mirages; the blue background,
light constructions of chance.

To hold back chaos I transformed
amorphous mass: clay, fire, or cloud,
so that the agéd gods might dance
and golden structures form.

I should have built, plain brick on brick,
a water tower. The sun flies on
arid wastes, barren hells too warm,
and me with a hazel stick!

Rivulets vanished in the dust
long ago, great compositions
vaporized, salt on the tongue so thick
that drinking, still I thirst.

Repeated desert, recurring drought,
sometimes hearing water trickle,
sometimes not, I, by doubting first,
believe; believing, doubt.

MICHAEL HAMBURGER

Arctic explorer

Whether dog will eat dog, likes boot leather frozen or boiled,
Whether walrus will prey on whale – the white or the grey? –
Or only on seal – the bearded or common? –
And is able in time to digest the clam swallowed whole;
Whether man can eat dog that has eaten the poisonous liver
Of polar bear, and wake up to indulge in a salad
Of sorrel and purple saxifrage after a breakfast of auks:
These were a few of the questions which if he did not answer
He probed as far as he could with his naked senses,
Knife-blade, bullet, harpoon, and the pain that probed him.
Fossils too he brought back and notes anthropologists noted –
The Eskimo's fear not of narwhal but bumble bee –
Temperature charts and rough maps of the nameless mountains,
Cures for frostbite and skills never dreamed of at home,
Never called for, either, never again to be used.

Brought back the knowledge that all his knowledge was loss;
And worse than loss, betrayal. Of musk-ox, of eiderduck?
Of gentle Eskimo? Soon to be anyone's game?
Them and more. Of the hard land unlocked by his loving
To procure for the pimps of empire another whore.
And wished he had brought back nothing, not even his body,
Left it to wolf or to fox, to the poppies' ravenous roots
Or only to glacier and silence, the diamond moonlight in
  winter.
Stayed there, died there in the first hard act.
Greater cold now he longed for, wider, more blizzard-swept
  skylines
For ever receding, crevasses more cunningly opening
And blindness the consummate vision, white, white to the point
  of blue,
Ice in his veins, and the snowlight burning to ice in his head.

Tides

To wake without fail when milk bottles shake in their racks,
Scrape one's face in the morning, every morning,
Take the same route to work and say 'good morning'
To the same row of scraped or powdered faces –
I cursed the roundness of this earth, I raged
At every self-perpetuating motion,
Hated the sea, that basher of dumb rock,
For all her factory of weeds and fishes,
The thumps, the thuds, the great reverberations –
Too much in rhythm; jarring, but by rote.

The metronome it was in my own head
That ticked and ticked; caged cricket in my head
That chirped and chirped until I had no ear
For syncopation, counterpoint of stillness
Beating against all music – of the sea,
Of birds and men, of season and machine,
Even of cricket and of metronome.
In silence I learned to listen; in the dark to look.

And unrepeatable now each morning's light
Modulates, shuffles, probes the daily faces
Often too suddenly different, like the street,
This weathered wall re-pointed, that new one cracked,
Apple trees that I prune while I forget
The shape of last year's boughs, cankered or grown,
And where that stump is, one that died in blossom;
Forget the hill's curve under the aerial masts.

No, wheels, grind on; seasons, repeat yourselves,
Milk bottles, rattle; familiars, gabble 'good morning';
Breed, hatch, digest your weeds and fishes, sea,
Omit no beat, nor rise to tidal waves.
Various enough the silences cut in
Between the rock cave's boom and the small wader's cry.

Homage to the weather

A tide, high tide of golden air.

Where, till this moment, were the bees?
And when no hum made for the honeysuckle,
Fumbled,
Became a body,
Clung and drank,
Spindrift, disowned, the petals hung,
And wait, let go was what the summer meant.

A corner of the garden, ivy on broken slats,
A branch with orange puffs: buddleia globosa.
Between two gusts a flood of golden air,
Mere hush, perhaps, abeyance – but the bees
Clinging and drinking.

Walls they brought with them: black courtyard in Paris,
A bit of marble, tumbled, dust on leaves,
A goldfish pond, the traffic not remote,
Audible, yet excluded;
Flowering tree or shrub in any weathered city,
Walls to contain a quietness, a quiver,
Fulfilment of the year, bees to be stilled.

Between two gusts, cold waves, the golden tide.

Mad lover, dead lady

Oh, my Diotima.
Is it not my Diotima you are speaking of?
Thirteen sons she bore me, one of them is Pope,
Sultan the next, the third is the Czar of Russia.
And do you know how it went with her?
Crazy, that's what she went, crazy, crazy, crazy.

Thirteen funerals they gave me when I died.
But she was not there. Locked up in a tower.
That's how it goes: round the bend
Out of the garden where lovers meet,
Walking, talking together. Over the wall.
No one there. Till you visitors come:
Will the corpse write a poem today
About his mad lady?

But I'll tell you a secret: we meet.
Round the bend, on the other side of the wall
Our garden is always there,
Easy, with every season's flowers.
Each from a dark street we come
And the sun shines.
She laughs when I tell her
What it's like to be dead.
I laugh when she gives me
News of our crazy children
Who've made their way in the world

No poem today, sir.
Go home. In a dream you'll see
How they remove themselves, your dead
Into madness. And seem to forget
Their loved ones, each in his own dark street.
How your mad loved ones
Seem to forget their dead.
That's how it goes. No one there.
Oh, my Diotima.
Waiting for me in the garden.

Psychosis

Where are you, girl, under the whole hulk
Of smooth flesh unused, the figurehead eyes
Pale blue enamel, staring, no laughter, no tears
To rise from within against lamplight, daylight

And refract them, playing?
Your lips are composed, for death.
When they part and the life in you finds a word
It is death, it is going down into sleep
And beyond, you're that far away, and there
You look for yourself.
                                        I look for you here,
Speak your name, beg you to stay, to wait,
For what, you ask, and I know
With electric currents they tore you
Out of your mad speed,
Joy of a kind, a fury, a pain,
And now with narcotics moor you
To where you are not.
                                        Why don't you die, is your answer,
As if there we could meet,
Or else to be rid of me
Trying to hold you, fighting
The undertow, tug of more than your weight
Together with it.
                                But where are you,
Where can I reach you with words,
With tongue or finger touch you and make you feel
So that you move again, if only to drift
With the water and winds that are passing you by?

It's your self-love you have lost,
Unloving, and I cannot serve it unloved.
Yet listen for once, tell me
What the place is like where diminished
You long to be less. Let the telling
Cut you loose for your own way.

CHRISTOPHER MIDDLETON

Gaunt man striding
(for *Jonathan Williams*)

Asperity. This rock
pins this hand; from
the other's palm air

spirits a cactus. Rock
heavy as habit. Cactus
throbs and shoots –

it is the pain, love
elemental, gnawing us
animal stars. Clamped,

from shoulder to toe
the body still can
thresh round, wrench.

To rise! You want
man striding, gaunt,
but nimble, dropping

gods in his furrow, now
his famous mushrooms, nights
bruising his great bones

on the desert grains. His
defiance! That being so,
here there is only a hand

under the rock and a hand
the cactus grows from.
To free these – how

burrow the one down
beyond the rock's root,
haul the other up, hose

the whole cactus through it –:
Jonathan Jonathan
keep your pain alive.

IAIN CRICHTON SMITH

Six poems

1.

You lived in Glasgow many years ago.
I do not find your breath in the air.
It was, I think, in the long-skirted thirties,
when idle men stood at every corner
chewing their fag-ends of a failed culture.
Now I sit here in George Square
where the War Memorial's yellow sword glows bright
and the white stone lions mouth at bus and car.
A maxi-skirted girl strolls slowly by.
I turn and look. It might be you. But no.
Around me there's a 1970 sky.

Everywhere there are statues. Stone remains.
The mottled flesh is transient. On those trams
invisible now but to the mind you bore
your groceries home to the 1930 slums.
'There was such warmth,' you said. The gaslight hums
and large caped shadows tremble on the stair.
Now everything is brighter. Pale ghosts walk
among the spindly chairs, the birchen trees.
In lights of fiercer voltage you are less
visible than when in winter you
walked, a black figure, through the gaslit blue.

The past's an experience that we cannot share.
Flat-capped Glaswegians and the Music Hall.
Apples and oranges on an open stall.
A day in the country. And the sparkling Clyde
splashing its local sewage at the wall.
The April day shakes memories in a shade
opening and shutting like a parasol.
There is no site for the unshifting dead.

You're buried elsewhere though your flickering soul
is a constant tenant of my tenement.

2.

Those who are needed do not easily die
or those who think they're needed. When your face
turned to the darkness it was as if the sky
took to itself its light. There were in space
no lightings from a God. No apples fell.
no new significance present to our slides
keeled from a distant planet, and no bell
swung anywhere one could hear. Or if it hides –
some heaven somewhere – with its level blue
and lack of gradient, it's beyond this ship
that through our atmosphere serenely glides
bearing intelligence and anguish too,
its natural pains, the honour that we keep
with ourselves, or heaven, or our compass guides.

3.

You told me once how your younger brother died.
It was by drowning. In the tar-black sea
he sang a psalm to bring his rescuers near.
That did not save him though. One cannot hide,
you would have said, from destiny. So here
there are two meanings working side by side.

You died of lack of oxygen. I tried
to fit the mask against your restless face
in the bumpy ambulance in which you lay.
I thought that moment of the psalm as guide,
beyond our vain technology, the grey
and scarlet blankets which you tossed aside.

4.

(On New Year's Morning, 1919, a ship called the *Iolaire*, bringing home ex-servicemen, was wrecked not far from Stornoway, its destination, drowning about three hundred men. The poem imagines a religious man, say an elder, standing by the shore on that morning, trying to work out what the tragedy means.)

The green washed over them. I saw them when
the New Year brought them home. It was a day
that orbed the horizon with an enigma.
It seemed that there were masts. It seemed that men
buzzed in the water round them. Logged they came
uniformed from the deep. It seemed that fire
shone in the water which was thin and white
unravelling towards the shore. It seemed that I
touched my fixed hat, which seemed to float and then
the sun illumined fish with naval caps,
names of the vanished ships. In sloppy waves,
in the fat of water, they came floating home
bruising against their island. It is true
I said to the ruining azure it is true
a minor error can inflict this death
that star is not responsible. It shone
over the puffy blouse, the flapping blue
trousers, the black boots. The seagulls swam
bonded to the water. Why not man?
The lights were lit last night, the tables creaked
with hoarded food. They willed the ship to port
in the New Year which would erase the old,
its errant voices, its unpractised tones.
Have we done ill, I ask. My sober hat
floated in the water, my fixed body
a simulacrum of the transient waste,
for everything was mobile, planks that swayed
the keeling ship exploding, and the splayed
cold insect bodies. I have seen your church
solid. This is not. The water pours
into the parting timbers where I ache

above the globular eyes. The slack heads turn
ringing the horizon without sound
with mortal bells, a strange exuberant flower
unknown to our dry churchyards. I look up.
The sky begins to brighten as before,
remorseless amber, and the bruised blue grows
at the erupting edges. The salty corps
come home together. I have known you, God,
not as the playful one but as the black
thunderer from hills. I've known you, God,
not as the playful one but as the stone
that desolates all knavery. I kneel
and touch this dumb blond bell. My hand is scorched.
Its human quality confuses me.

I have not felt such hair so dear before
nor seen such real eyes. I kneel from you.
This water soaks me. I am running with
its tart sharp joy. Lord, I am floating here
in my black uniform. I am embraced
by these green ignorant waters. I am calm.

5.

The politicians gesture in this bland
and azure summer, superficies
of the mind slumbering in its folded leaves.

None shall speak of the black implacable star
beyond the manifestoes of the day
that's unappeased by buttonhole or rose.

As if the floating vote should Charon's boat
guide with its souls to a benignant heaven
those dim majorities on the other side

and none shall mention that rotating vase
constituent of no politics but made
not out of speech but silence and rich shade.

6.

He said: We argue and we come to this,
Dostoevsky saying everything is allowed
if there is no continuance after death.
If all the answers have material faces
and no one sees the fine spiritual graces
descending from the heavens in luminous dress
then there's the terror of pure nothingness.

The laws of God engraved on tablets were
pure as the morning, for their authorship
was that which made the morning after all.
The azure and the stone both came together
in a perfected and benignant weather.
The tablets were originals of the air
and made it mean exactly what we are.

If behind the morning there are no
immortal birds parading, if behind
the stubborn stone there isn't more than stone
how shall we find direction? As the hum
of bees in summer harmonises plum
and grape and apple so that these are notes
inside the music which so dominates

the else unmeaning scenery; as in art
the poet knows when he's concluded, for
there's an exactitude that he's aiming at.
He knows it by a sense beyond the poem,
he knows it as he knows a coming home,
perfection to which nothing can be added
nor by the mind can wholly be decoded.

As even translating from one language to
another one a residue remains,
there is a gap electricity can't leap.
So words remain ungathered (harvests too)
if that is all that words or harvests do,
that is, just mean themselves and do not point
to a certain place where both of them are joined.

Everything is allowable, said the Russian,
if death is all there is, if we should stay
fixed to that body, empty as a vase
which once held life but now is merely clay,
an object without meaning in our day
of living fish and dogs. That rats should have
their sly quick purpose, their malignant grave

radiance and expression, and you none!
It cannot be that this phenomenon
should disappear as water from a jar.
The world is so impregnated with mind
there must exist a mode at which we find
conversions occurring, like as the caterpillars
transformed to moths of an angelic colour.

The Greeks believed the circle was the perfect
figure. Therefore the heavens must conform.
There had to be a way to make ellipses
respectable and so explain the orbit
of planets moving gravely through the light.
It just required a little movement of
a human mind, a justice as of love.

So from a certain stance (as if backstage)
I see the transformation, how a dull
loggish stability becomes the quick
and brilliant foil which lights a whole stage up,
how from a dreary ordinary sleep
lights flash in all directions from pure faces
which are as diamonds in their clear excesses.

Or as in spring an acre becomes blue
and there are bluebells shining mile on mile,
vivid creation of the dullest earth.
Or as in genius ordinary words appear
angelic, peasant becomes peer,
brown wears the purple, and from hedges flower
whole detonations of remarkable power.

O there are moments when a certain star
rising over the waters is a song

a glove, a perfume, a remembrancer,
a soul steadily rising or a 'star',
a spiritual Garbo near and far,
a private public being whom the earth
cannot wholly hide though it gave her birth.

I sense a vast connection, spiritual things
bodying forth material, material too
bodying forth the spiritual, so I know
that death is just a place that we have looked
too deeply at, not into, as at a book
held just that inch too close. For we must hold
back from a painting just to see it whole.

And what was blurred becomes quite ordered then,
out of the chaos marches a whole street
with a church, an inn, and houses, people too,
and the light curves all around them with the shape
of a woman in her vulnerable hope
bent over a cradle, tucking sheet and shawl
into an order which is loved and real.

ROY FISHER

Seven attempted moves

If the night were not so dark
  this would be seen
Deep red,
  the last red before black.
Beside the soft earth steps,
  a wall of heaped stones
Breathes and
  flowers
    and breathes.

*

A cast concrete basin
  with a hole in the bottom
Empty but for
  a drift of black grit
Some feathers some hair
  some grey paper.
Nothing else for the puzzled face to see.

*

Crisis –
  a man should be able
To hope for a well made crisis,
Something to brace against.
But see it come in rapidly and mean
  along some corridor
In a pauperous civic Office.

*

Under the portico
Huge-winged shadows
  hang

Brown
  with a scent
    of powdered
Leather.
Up the steps
  into this
Depth. Recession.
  Promise of star-scratched dark.
Then put your ear to the door;
  listen
As in a shell
  to the traffic
Slithering along behind it.

*

Here are the schoolroom chairs on which
  the ministers, in the playground,
Sat to be shot.
  Four chairs; the property
Of the Department of Education;
Stolen
  the same night
By this souvenir hunter
  with his respect for neither side –
Just for things happening;
  then sought in vain
And after a long while
  written off the books
Of the Department of Education.

*

Bright birchleaves, luminous and orange,
Stick after six months to the street,
  trodden down:
Now as at every minute perfect.

*

It is a shame.
  There is
    nowhere to go.

Doors into further in
  lead out already
To new gardens
Small enough for pets' droppings
  quickly to cover:
Ceilings
  too soon, steps curtailed;
The minibed; minibath;
  and jammed close
    the minican.
Confinement,
  shortness of breath.
Only a state of mind,
  And
Statues of it built everywhere.

For 'realism'

For 'realism':
the sight of Lucas's
lamp factory on a summer night;
a shift coming off about nine,
pale light, dispersing,
runnels of people chased
by pavements drying off
quickly after them,
away among the wrinkled
brown houses
where there are cracks for them to go;

sometimes
at the corner of Farm
and Wheeler Streets, standing in that
stained, half-deserted place –

pale light for staring up
four floors high
through the blind window walls
of a hall of engines,

shady humps left alone,
no lights on in there
except the sky –

there presses in,
and not as conscience,
what concentrates in the warm hollow:
movements at doors, clothes,
whitish grey, dry; open foodshops;
people going about constantly but not far:
man with a suit,
facing into a corner, straddling,
keeping his shoes dry. Women step,
talking, over the stream; he answers the men
who call out as they go by.
Above, dignity. A new precinct
comes over the scraped hill;
flats on the ridge get the last light;

down Wheeler Street, the lamps
already gone, the windows have
lake-stretches of silver
gashed out of tea-green shadows,
the after-images of brickwork.

A conscience
builds, late, on the ridge. A realism
tries to record, before they're gone
what silver filth these drains have run.

Five morning poems from a picture by Manet

1.

Wells of shadow by the stream
And the long branches
High over pools of gold light in the grass.

A drift of morning-scents
Downward through pines,
Dazzled, to hang on water finally;
The road's deserted curve: beyond,
Blue town-smoke standing.

Schoolboy in the scarlet cap,
Leaning across the wall
Motionless –
Will you feel the moment end,
A dead scale sliding from a fish?

Plain-featured boy, cast in a pose of beauty.

Wells of shadow spread the stream
So dark it glides invisibly
Between his dabbling fingers
And leaves his coat-cuff dry.

Slant eyes that shine too deep a brown
To show time, or to tell
What tautens
Stillness round him to a fine
Film that shivers, glazed and sombre:

The scents, maybe, that sting

Or ironstone in the water, the taste of April.

So dark it glides invisibly
The moment takes its form
Out of his smile, that rests on turbulence –
There have been tears, there could be greed.

Someone has given him cherries:
Untouched upon the wall
They spill from yellow paper, crimson-heavy;
Glossy, their soft skins burst.

High over light-pools in the grass
And still boughs, a bronze shadow
Gestures behind my dream,
A god, polished to nothing by our thoughts:

Plenitude, rising at the heart's pace to noon,
That shadow turns clear waterglass of light
To amber, and extinguishes
The last white flecks of agitation.

Music of the generous eye,
Swelling, receding on my breath.

Here are the golden distances;
Deeper than life the stream goes in the shade.

Cool trees. Clarity. Dreaming boy.
Fat cherries and a scarlet cap;
Water under the thin smoke of morning –

Music of the generous eye.

2.

Nowhere. Hear the stormy spring
Far off across the racks of quiet. Nothing.
Suddenly, a leaning fence-post daubed with rain.

It rots into the day. Cold lights
Swell from the clouds, then take their death away.

Some ceremony lets fall its links:
A glistening fence-post suddenly encountered;

Iron trumpets in the sky.

All in the flooded meadow, ankle-deep,
The lately dead, the tidy men and women
Walking with steps like flakes of agony.

Accurate as the trumpet notes they go,
With polished shoes in the gunmetal water;
They tread on loss as once they counted money.

All in the meadow. Flakes of agony
Walk with cut marble steps to iron trumpets.

Ceremony to wear away the world.

Barbaric news for someone about to die:
Each footfall muffles breath, each iron grace-note
Stoppers the heart with heartless beauty.

A world freezing apart, where a movement
Cracks the glass veins of music in the flesh.

Islands of understanding float, confused:
Rain-smears on rotting wood, the sheepish dead
Who stand amid the floods, bright stems of glass
Shattering by inches; lakes of misery

The iron trumpets wear away the sky.

3.

Death music sounds for a boy by a stream,
Urgent as waves, as polished shoes,
Though amber screens of light shade him from time.

Ironstone in the water, tasting
Coldly of April pleasure yet
Embitters like brass the pools of golden morning.

Trumpets of iron shake the sky;
In chains of ceremony they spill
Out of the music of a generous eye.

Over his quiet they wear away
All to a frigid emphasis
On lines that form his child's flesh into beauty.

Slowly comes the polished step,
Cut marble agony to blight
The charm of cherries and the scarlet cap;

To drag the forms of beauty till they gleam
Dully on lakes of misery
Rising from wells of shadow by the stream.

4.

Looking for life, I lost my mind:
Only the dead
Spoke through their yellow teeth
Into the marble tombs they lay beneath,
Splinters of fact stuck in the earth's fat rind.

The privet glittered with noon; the hill
Slid its green head
Down from the sky to try me. I was still
As the evil-shaped dark leaves.
Then I heard what the corpses said.

Muttering, they told me how their lives
From burial
Spiked back at the world like knives
Striking at the past for bad legacies –
The fiction of understanding worst of all.

I saw a vase of familiar flowers,
Behind it, a tray,
Of pale thin brass with patterned borders;
The troubling taste of an alien mouth not figured
Even in fantasy.

5.

Walking beside the wall towards the stream
Where flickering water-lights
Lick amber tongues quickly across stone,
With a yellow bag of cherries, an old jacket,
A red cap crumpled on thick hair,
Thought, an uneven slime;
Gravel underfoot; the wall's rough edge;
Stub fingers sliding over the pads of moss.

Stout morning walls the sun walks down,
Smoke bursting slow into invisibility,
The tight sky broken among banks of trees;

Sounds vanishing through worn patches on the road,
Dark silence dropping from the ledges of the pines.

Flat heads of stone amid the turf. The shadowy stream.

Continuity

In a covered way along the outside of the building,
A glazed lean-to with the panes painted over,
There's nothing but the light, falling across the quarries
From the lamp in the wall above.

Purpose? No purpose. Apparitions? None.
Where the lamplight peters out across the yard
Two shallow plant pots swim the night.

There is smoke folded into the waters,
The fish-trap gives the waters form,
Minimal form, drawn on the current, unattended,
The lure and the check. So much free water.

Long clouds are lined
Over the level-crossing ramp.
Faces behind car-glass painted with reflection,
Pressed in the seats, warm bodies;
And the exhausts patter on the dirt
Stained through with oils, sterile with gases.

When they pull away across the ballast
Dirty Nature claims her own.

Tongues of grease in rings of light.

The towns are endless as the waters are.

The making of the book

'Let the Blurb be strong,
Modest, and true.
Build it to take a belting;
They'll pick on that.

Then choose your second gang –
The first, led by your publisher,
You already belong to,
Its membership involuntary, if free –

For the other, set up an interesting
Tension between the acknowledgements
And the resemblances; but in the photograph keep
The cut of your moustache equivocal.

Write your own warrant. Make plain
In idiot-sized letters
For which of the others you'll take the blame – Yes:
It's *necessary* to belong;

Several allegiances
Are laid out for you ready.
And remember, though you're only a poet,
There's somebody, somewhere, whose patience

It falls to *you* finally to exhaust.
For poetry, we have to take it, is essential
Though menial; its purpose
Constantly to set up little enmities.

Faction makes a reciprocal
To-and-fro of the simplest sort – and characterless
But for an 'aesthetic' variable,
Inaudible to all but the players.

And this little mindless motion,
That nobody but the selfless and schooled-
For-Service would ever stoop to,
Drives the Society.

It's a long story:
But the minuscule dialectic,
Tick-tacking away, no more than notional,
In obscure columns,

At length transmits itself
Mysteriously through Education –
Which pays off the poets too,
One way and another –

Out beyond Government,
Past Control and Commodity
Even to the hollowness
Of the seventeenth percentile, the outermost
Reaches of the responsible.

If the reviewers fall idle, everybody drops dead:
It's as simple as that.

– *Go, little book.*'

JON SILKIN

A word about freedom and identity in Tel-Aviv

Through a square sealed-off with
a grey & ornate house,
its length bent, for one corner of that,
a road leads off, got to down steps:
wide, terraced, ample.
The road's quiet, too; but nudges as
the square did not. Walking
some, below the city I heard
a pared, harsh cry, sustained
and hovering, between outrage
and despair; scraped by itself
into a wedge-shape opening on
inaccessibly demented hurt
it can't since quite come at;
imitative, harsh, genuine.
A pet-shop four feet below
pavement level; in its front yard
a blue parrot, its open beak
hooked and black, the folded wings
irregularly lifting a little;
under which, dull yellow soft plumage,
the insides of itself, heaved slightly.
Its tail was long, stiff. Long in stiffness
that at once bends entirely
if bent too much. And as it
turned in its cage, bending the tail
against the wires, it spoke
into the claw it raised
at its hooked face, the word
'toràh, toràh'* in the hoarse, devotional

*The Toràh consists of the teaching, instruction, and judicial decisions, given by the ancient Hebrew priests as a revelation of the Divine will.

grief religious men speak with
rendering on God the law
their love binds them with. Done,
it cried its own cry, its claws tightening
onto its beak, shaking slowly
the whole face with the cry
from side to side. This cry was placed by
one Jew inside another. Not belonging though;
an animal of no distinct race,
its cry also human, slightly;
wired in, waiting; fed on
good seed a bit casually
planted. Granulated, sifted,
dry. The toràh is:
suffering begets suffering, that is.

Worm

Look out, they say, for yourself.
The worm doesn't. It is blind
As a sloe; its death by cutting,
Bitter. Its oozed length is ringed,
With parts swollen. Cold and blind
It is graspable, and writhes
In your hot hand; a small snake, unvenomous.
Its seeds furred and moist
It sexes by lying beside another,
In its eking conjunction of seed
Wriggling and worm-like.
Its ganglia are in its head,
And if this is severed
It must grow backwards.
It is lowly, useful, pink. It breaks
Tons of soil, gorging the humus
Its whole length; its shit a fine cast
Coiled in heaps, a burial mound, or like a shell

Made by a dead snail.
It has a life, which is virtuous
As a farmer's, making his own food.
Passionless as a hoe, sometimes, persistent.
Does not want to kill a thing.

Divisions

Cedars from Lebanon, in community, move into the swart,
pointed hills.
I don't say many. On two legs bound into one,
rooted into terraces between drops of rock-face, in sparse soils
cornered where wind pushed that. Layers of snapping pointed
stone shift,
one can guess, like whelpings, about their roots.
These roots know what they are about. The trees came together,
tall, fleshed like a wax feather,
their leaves green throughout. And as the sun changes the trees
don't; sharp, slim.
Not many know what sex these creatures are made of.
The whole tree comes into the folded integral hills
of Judah, one of many, towards a sea struggling
to erode from the land its form into the shape of Africa.
Creatures with two legs come, and sit against a Cedar that no
longer moves
forward. They spread a map over their legs, engross a frontier;
a document embossed by lines that divide one bit of land from
the same bit,
the first of these trees from the last of them. The line is
arbitrary as a fish-hook. As if two iron hooks
stuck like picks into the ground, and their shafts pulled,
until in the earth a gap opened. A small, neat structure of stones,
in fact, marks the hostile step which it is death to step.
Judah's hills do not stoop, they are said to skip; those trees
in Lebanon do not bend; their mild, emulsive
sharpnesses advance through the nourishing earth they compact.
A hexagon of dirt is trapped back by a leaf into the soil.

Suddenly the landscape, one might say, is startled by
a man in a blue shirt, its greens, its ochres fixed by a depth of blue;
as if before these changed but now were frozen by the quality of blue that they are not.
He crouches; what is he speaking to the wrinkled olive; what disdain
for the tree's agedness as the plucked creature furs its oil on his salt fingers?
The hills shimmer; also, the tree standing in them: a trembling on one
point from inside. A haze, in dots, condenses over the contracted earth.
Past that tree, there, that shorter one, two men are dead.
The sun is pushing off, the trees persist inside their shade
eating deeply on the earth. Opening the clothes you see
among the groiny hair, the useful penis, in the heat distended slightly.
One of the men's has a head, circumcised; a chin, a ridge
that visibly hardened as its body's blood gathered to it intently.
Alive, a bit of marble with a ruff of skin, in folds; thin, brown, slack.
The other man's is hooded. Each had its fissure that as it entered it
the lips folded back upon themselves, the ground moistening its entrance.
Now the vulva, slightly swollen, its hair local, remains closed however.
The lips closed, in a pained sleep: the female part ruminant.
No: the female part mourns the unique instrument it was to it.
The faces of the men show that death, which each divided on the other's
body, entered the left ear, and then the mouth. In leisure.
None attends them. The sabbath intervenes like a blade.

Spade

George Culley, Isaac Greener?

A want of sound hangs
in a drop of moisture from the wheel that
turned and washed the ore.

A rustling of clothes on the wind. The water does not move.

I have come here to be afraid.
I came for love to bundle
what was mine. I am scared
to sneak into the hut to find your coat.

When you put down your pick,
when others wouldn't sprag
the mine's passages; when you said no:

soldiers, who do not strike,
thrust
their bayonets into you.

They were told to.

The young mayor, shitting, closeted
with chain on his neck. I want to

push my hands into your blood
because I caused you to use yours.

I did not die; love, I did not. All the parts
of England fell melting like lead away,
as you showed me the melting once, when you and the men
with you were jabbed,

and without tenderness, were filled over;
no psalm, leaf-like, shading the eyelid
as the eye beneath is dazed abruptly
in the earth's flare of black light
burning after death.

The spade digging in the sunlight illuminates the face of my
God.
Blind him.

Flatfish

1.

It moves vertically through salted
Pressures, with a head that sees sideways.
The nets are submerged, which it enters.
Nothing to come for specially. Men want it.

The white flesh powered by a tail filmed with skin
Sways its mild hulk into their fold.
The white flesh is food. When boiled,
It flakes easily off the bone.

Is this love? God created us
For the toothed shark, the molestation
of two jaws hinged through flesh
Onto each other's hooked teeth.

Its ethics are formal, determined.
Otherwise He made the mild flatfish,
And gleaning mackerel that fatten
On the dead's helplessness strengthening its rancid colours.

He made the flatfish, their eyes
Naive as a bead drawn from a leopard's skin.
Their white flesh is flaked into the mossy,
Acidic belly, just hanging.

The good salt, phosphate, each dissolved
Into flesh. The fish are left to gasp
In ships' holds, mulcting the air
For air moving in the gill's membrane

Miserly, useless. A gradual pain
Until the fish weaken. Could they cry
We might gas them to concert
Their distress. Nets are men's media,

Their formal, knotted, rectangular intelligence.
They survive on what the fish weighs, their welfare
Accurate as a pair of scales.

2.

We are not going to change.
But husband the sea, planting the fish spawn in
The frigid heft of plot-water
Grey, but not stone.

Mackerel will gorge
A sea parsley, its flowers sprinkled with a white, granular petal;
The shark will eat mud
At the sea's foundation.

Though to reap will be by net,
As many fish as grains husked from their flattened case,
The ear raped of its oval bolus
Folded into itself.

The precise allotment of fish
A growth in kind; pollination by a brush tasked
Onto differing species
For the flesh's good.

The flesh's good. Elsewhere
We seized on our own kind, not for food. Each fish
Glides through a forest,
An oily lung

Of sea weed, the swell
Moved in a land-grafted integument of sea plant. A uniform
Thicket moon-masted, its foliage
Begins to lock

Fast with sea-forester's
Skill. We evolve with our hands and brain. The pad of each
Hand, moist; the nails sharp
As a grown fin.

ALAN BROWNJOHN

A teacher of the deaf

(for *C.E.*)

Her purpose is to mould words for them, wholly
Out of the ordinary sight of things, make meanings
To link and connect with objects, to effect communication.
And from their silent country they stretch out
Their wordless thought to her indicating lips, they grasp
Aspects of movement in her face, and make them
Symbols for things themselves, in their feeling sense.

An object is the easiest. Think of *cat*,
The living animal that is, and moves;
(*Is*, of course, is a difficult word; existence
Is no simple attribute.) Yet, incidentally,
Think can be, surprisingly, quite quickly taught.
Thinking, somehow, can be told, or shown, or mimed –
A hand at the head, an expression, then an action.

But only slowly come the classes of things –
So easily confused with the things themselves.
Three cats will not mean *animal* in kind, but only *cats*.
And numbers, though they grasp them, do not help here;
They do not define, but merely multiply *cat*.
Or adjectives will be mistaken for what they describe:
Black cat seems *cat*, a *heavy* book – just *book*.

Yet these are the foothills of her mountain.
On steeper slopes come *for* and *to* and *the*,
Articles, and prepositions of place. These are confused
With the actions done in teaching them. For example,
I walk to the door: walk and *door* are easily learnt,
But *to* and *the* slip by Her patient lips
Convey a movement, but no meaning stirs.

Some means must be found and used, by way of signs,
To create the elusive sense of such expressions,
That the climbers might move on from the seen and known, and
Up to the strange, invisible *idea*. She will have to make actions

Seem to possess a meaning beyond the facts
And subtler than the movement. She will have to come
At last to the hardest in the range of word and thought,

The unseen abstract, content of mind alone.
This is an escarpment for her. What is *real*? *Unreal*?
Or what is *wise*? Or *foolish*? *Good*? Or *bad*?
But once beyond that, the mountain can be viewed
From its highest point: and her sense can be comprehended.
She has now to begin to point out the extended land,
For they, with this summit reached, can *understand*.

GEOFFREY HILL

Funeral music

William de la Pole, Duke of Suffolk: beheaded 1450
John Tiptoft, Earl of Worcester: beheaded 1470
Anthony Woodville, Earl Rivers: beheaded 1483

1.

Processionals in the exemplary cave,
Benediction of shadows. Pomfret. London.
The voice fragrant with mannered humility,
With an equable contempt for this World,
'In honorem Trinitatis'. Crash. The head
Struck down into a meaty conduit of blood.
So these dispose themselves to receive each
Pentecostal blow from axe or seraph,
Spattering block-straw with mortal residue.
Psalteries whine through the empyrean. Fire
Flares in the pit, ghosting upon stone
Creatures of such rampant state, vacuous
Ceremony of possession, restless
Habitation, no man's dwelling-place.

2.

For whom do we scrape our tribute of pain –
For none but the ritual king? We meditate
A rueful mystery; we are dying
To satisfy fat Caritas, those
Wiped jaws of stone. (Suppose all reconciled
By silent music; imagine the future
Flashed back at us, like steel against sun,
Ultimate recompense.) Recall the cold
Of Towton on Palm Sunday before dawn,
Wakefield, Tewkesbury: fastidious trumpets
Shrilling into the ruck; some trampled

Acres, parched, sodden or blanched by sleet,
Stuck with strange-postured dead. Recall the wind's
Flurrying, darkness over the human mire.

3.

They bespoke doomsday and they meant it by
God, their curved metal rimming the low ridge.
But few appearances are like this. Once
Every five hundred years a comet's
Over-riding stillness might reveal men
In such array, livid and featureless,
With England crouched beastwise beneath it all.
'Oh, that old northern business . . .' A field
After battle utters its own sound
Which is like nothing on earth, but is earth.
Blindly the questing snail, vulnerable
Mole emerge, blindly we lie down, blindly
Among carnage the most delicate souls
Tup in their marriage-blood, gasping 'Jesus'.

4.

Let mind be more precious than soul; it will not
Endure. Soul grasps its price, begs its own peace,
Settles with tears and sweat, is possibly
Indestructible. That I can believe.
Though I would scorn the mere instinct of faith,
Expediency of assent, if I dared,
What I dare not is a waste history
Or void rule. Averroes, old heathen,
If only you had been right, if Intellect
Itself were absolute law, sufficient grace,
Our lives could be a myth of captivity
Which we might enter: an unpeopled region
Of ever new-fallen snow, a palace blazing
With perpetual silence as with torches.

5.

As with torches we go, at wild Christmas,
When we revel in our atonement
Through thirty feasts of unction and slaughter,
What is that but the soul's winter sleep?
So many things rest under consummate
Justice as though trumpets purified law,
Spikenard were the real essence of remorse.
The sky gathers up darkness. When we chant
'Ora, ora pro nobis' it is not
Seraphs who descend to pity but ourselves.
Those righteously-accused those vengeful
Racked on articulate looms indulge us
With lingering shows of pain, a flagrant
Tenderness of the damned for their own flesh:

6.

My little son, when you could command marvels
Without mercy, outstare the wearisome
Dragon of sleep, I rejoiced above all –
A stranger well-received in your kingdom.
On those pristine fields I saw humankind
As it was named by the Father; fabulous
Beasts rearing in stillness to be blessed.
The world's real cries reached there, turbulence
From remote storms, rumour of solitudes,
A composed mystery. And so it ends.
Some parch for what they were; others are made
Blind to all but one vision, their necessity
To be reconciled. I believe in my
Abandonment, since it is what I have.

7.

'Prowess, vanity, mutual regard,
It seemed I stared at them, they at me.
That was the gorgon's true and mortal gaze:

Averted conscience turned against itself.'
A hawk and a hawk-shadow. 'At noon,
As the armies met, each mirrored the other;
Neither was outshone. So they flashed and vanished
And all that survived them was the stark ground
Of this pain. I made no sound, but once
I stiffened as though a remote cry
Had heralded my name. It was nothing . . .'
Reddish ice tinged the reeds; dislodged, a few
Feathers drifted across; carrion birds
Strutted upon the armour of the dead.

8.

Not as we are but as we must appear,
Contractual ghosts of pity; not as we
Desire life but as they would have us live,
Set apart in timeless colloquy:
So it is required; so we bear witness,
Despite ourselves, to what is beyond us,
Each distant sphere of harmony forever
Poised, unanswerable. If it is without
Consequence when we vaunt and suffer, or
If it is not, all echoes are the same
In such eternity. Then tell me, love,
How that should comfort us – or anyone
Dragged half-unnerved out of this worldly place,
Crying to the end 'I have not finished'.

Funeral Music
an essay

In this sequence I was attempting a florid grim music broken by grunts and shrieks. Ian Nairn's description of Eltham Palace as 'a perfect example of the ornate heartlessness of much mid-fifteenth-century architecture, especially court architecture'[1] is pertinent,

1. Ian Nairn, *Nairn's London*, (Penguin 1966), p. 208.

though I did not read Nairn until after the sequence had been completed. The Great Hall was made for Edward IV. *Funeral Music* could be called a commination and an alleluia for the period popularly but inexactly known as the Wars of the Roses. It bears an oblique dedication. In the case of Suffolk the word 'beheaded' is a retrospective aggrandisement; he was in fact butchered across the gunwale of a skiff. Tiptoft enjoyed a degree of ritual, commanding that he should be decapitated in three strokes 'in honour of the Trinity'. This was a nice compounding of orthodox humility and unorthodox arrogance. Did Tiptoft see himself as Everyman's emblem or as the unique figure preserved in the tableau of his own death? As historic characters Suffolk, Worcester and Rivers haunt the mind vulnerable alike to admiration and scepticism. Was Suffolk – the friend of the captive poet Charles d'Orléans and an advocate of peace with France – a visionary or a racketeer? The Woodville clan invites irritated dismissal: pushful, time-serving, it was really not its business to produce a man like Earl Rivers, who was something of a religious mystic and whose translation, *The Dictes and Sayings of the Philosophers*, was the first book printed in England by Caxton. Suffolk and Rivers were poets, though quite tame. Tiptoft, patron of humanist scholars, was known as the Butcher of England because of his pleasure in varying the accepted postures of judicial death.

Admittedly, the sequence avoids shaping these characters and events into any overt narrative or dramatic structure. The whole inference, though, has value if it gives a key to the ornate and heartless music punctuated by mutterings, blasphemies and cries for help.

There is a distant fury of battle. Without attempting factual detail, I had in mind the Battle of Towton, fought on Palm Sunday, 1461. It is now customary to play down the violence of the Wars of the Roses and to present them as dynastic skirmishes fatal, perhaps, to the old aristocracy but generally of small concern to the common people and without much effect on the economic routines of the kingdom. Statistically, this may be arguable; imaginatively, the Battle of Towton itself commands one's belated witness. In the accounts of the contemporary chroniclers it was a holocaust. Some scholars have suggested that the claims were exaggerated, although the military historian, Colonel A. H. Burne, argues convincingly for the reasonableness of the early estimates. He reckons that over twenty-six thousand men died at Towton and remarks that 'the scene must have beggared description and its very horror probably deterred the survivors from passing on stories of the fight'.[2] Even so, one finds the chronicler of Croyland Abbey writing that the blood of the slain lay caked with the snow which covered the ground and that, when the snow melted, the blood flowed along the furrows and ditches for a distance of two or three miles.[3]

Locust songs
(to *Allan Seager*)

The emblem

So with sweet oaths converting the salt earth
To yield, our fathers verged on Paradise:
Each to his own portion of Paradise,
Stung by the innocent venoms of the earth.

Good husbandry

Out of the foliage of sensual pride
Those teeming apples! Summer burned well
The dramatic flesh; made work for pride
Forking into the tender mouths of Hell

Heaped windfalls, pulp for the Gadarene
Squealers. This must be our reward:
To smell God writhing over the rich scene.
Gluttons for wrath, we stomach our reward.

2. A. H. Burne, *The Battlefields of England*, (Methuen 1950), p. 100.
3. Cited by C. R. Markham, *Yorkshire Archaeological and Topographical Journal*, vol. 10 (1889), p. 13.

Shiloh Church, 1862: twenty-three thousand

O stamping-ground of the shod Word! So hard
On the heels of the damned red-man we came,
Geneva's tribe, outlandish and abhorred –
Bland vistas milky with Jehovah's calm –

Who fell to feasting Nature, the glare
Of buzzards circling; cried to the grim sun
'Jehovah punish us!'; who went too far;
In deserts dropped the odd white turds of bone;

Whose passion was to find out God in this
His natural filth, voyeur of sacrifice: a slow
Bloody unearthing of the God-in-us.
But with what blood, and to what end, Shiloh?

September song

born 19.6.32 – deported 24.9.42

Undesirable you may have been, untouchable
you were not. Not forgotten
or passed over at the proper time.

As estimated, you died. Things marched,
sufficient, to that end.
Just so much Zyklon and leather, patented
terror, so many routine cries.

(I have made
an elegy for myself it
is true)

September fattens on vines. Roses
flake from the wall. The smoke
of harmless fires drifts to my eyes.

This is plenty. This is more than enough.

A song from Armenia

Roughly-silvered leaves that are the snow
On Ararat seen through those leaves.
The sun lays down a foliage of shade.

A drinking-fountain pulses its head
Two or three inches from the troughed stone.
An old woman sucks there, gripping the rim.

Why do I have to relive, even now,
Your mouth, and your hand running over me
Deft as a lizard, like a sinew of water?

The Assisi fragments

(to *G. Wilson Knight*)

1.

Lion and lioness, the mild
Inflammable beasts,
At their precise peril kept
Distance and repose –
And there the serpent
Innocently shone its head.

2.

So the hawk had its pursuit. So Death
Opened its childish eyes. So the angels
Overcame Adam: he was defiled
By balm. Creator, and creature made
Of unnatural earth, he howled
To the raven *find me*; to the wolf
Eat, my brother; and to the fire *I am clean.*

GEORGE MACBETH

Cranach's hunts

On the first afternoon
they go out of the white city
into the wood.

One with a flat
red hat
has a feathered neck
on his lance.

One with a black hat
is upon a doe
with his sheathed sword.

In the folded
grey sheets of the river
the stags are dying.

Branched heads
waver like water-weeds.

On the bank
seven dogs
beset a hooped one.

Thrown as if
by a tree
one lies in a mat
of its own blood.

In a nearby boat
ladies in long dresses
are rowing.

One is being
groped
by a friar.

The spire of
the church
and the blue peak
assure the world
of a fine day.

After all, the king is hunting.

On the second afternoon
they have crossed the
bridge
and are in the firs

with their white swords
erect.

Head down
a stag
is already
under their hooves.

The tongues
of the dogs
flicker
over its body.

In threshed
water
the rest
move their
crowns of thorns.

Today
the ladies
make the shapes of breasts
with their bows.

The church
is nowhere to be seen.

Far off,
the city is roofed in blood.

In a green clearing
all the does in the world
walk naked
before a serving-man
in a grey helmet.

The light
still glistens in their pupils.

The date is 1544.

It might have been yesterday.

ANSELM HOLLO

The Empress Hotel poems

1.

Just get up
and sit down again. Then
    you can watch the dust
        settle.
Or wait for the Irishman to come round
knock on your door again. Twice
    he's asked me
first, the time, and then
'Would you know of anyplehs I could get a job sirr –
    lehborin', that is.'
They won't take him, he looks too
purgatorial. Poor soul
8 days over from Eire
        where they have strikes.

2.

The typewriter banging
better than radio   for company.
Sheets of translation pile up. Too many
    words, too many
other men's words
    bang thru my head. Why don't they learn English
in Finland. Why don't they learn Finnish Swedish German
    in England, Old & New.
They're just being kind to you, Anselm.
    They don't learn,
        you earn.

3.

The old housekeeper lady downstairs
likes the stamps. She says Could you
let me have them if you're going to throw them away
anyway. Mr Burroughs she says
always did that, he always
gave me the stamps. He got a lot of
mail, too.
I give them to her. We are
Burroughs Hollo Saarikoski Ball
we are Mrs Hardy's
nice writing gentlemen.

4.

White smoke from Battersea Power Station
rises moon star London city light
beam from the Airport
sweeps the sky. I switch the room light
on and off and on, light dark light dark.
It occurs to me
I'm trying to tell you
what goes on inside me.
Out there
they'll suspect
a Chinese spy.
Ha. Battersea Beast on its back
pushing vapor puffs thru the soles of its feet
for fun.

5.

Go thru my things
god knows what you'll find. When I'm not here.
I'm not here, in this poem
I'm in another room, writing praises
of their loveliness and terror
the long-haired beings that dance thru my mind
not endlessly, but to be one, at one
with them
I want to be.
I want to be one,
I want her to be one.
When the voice begins
she is, and she dances.
I am the voice. I praise.
There is
no mind.

6.

To return and find
2 men in grey suits who have come to look at me thru their eyes
and say Mr H. is this yours? you know they're illegal
in this country. Oh I didn't know.
Well they are, you better get rid of it. OK.
They go, and I think
it is a good thing to have more than one room.
What would they say
if they found what I have
in the other poem.

TED WALKER

Cuckoo-pint

So cold now. I remember
you – bright hedgerow tarts you were,
flagrant in your big red beads,
cheerful, vulgar and brazen.
But then

in a sudden October
when the white night of winter
came, you put aside your gauds
and took vows. Now you open
again,

hooded, cool and sinister.
I know you for what you are
unveiled: loose, secular brides
frustrated with this convent
torment.

Terrains vagues

At the edge of any town,
at the edge of any life
are tracts we never build on;
ragged wildernesses, half-
wild, unkempt and overgrown.
They're easy to return from,

and there is no risk. Children
gipsies, lovers, tramps, all go there
to do what they must: and none
can come to harm, save when we're
there too. For we infect them
by our coming. When we stare

at them, steal a turf or two,
litter them with what we've felt,
they are soiled by what we do
and they watch us with our guilt.

Grebe

Today the April winds blow
in the tippets of your crest;
the waves are hard beneath you,
as by your will. And you stand
wide-winged like a little Christ
using the water like land.

I can forget the mammal
that I am for days; and though
in the womb I was reptile,
fish, I have no memory
of the scales I shed, and no
sense of the gekko in me.

But you – are you going back
to be again what once you were
before your ancestors shook
their first wet feathers and flew
into the alien air
you find so alien now?

TONY HARRISON

The nuptial torches

These human victims, chained and burning at the stake, were the blazing torches which lighted the monarch to his nuptial couch.

J. L. Motley, The Rise of the Dutch Republic

Fish gnaw the Flushing capons, hauled from fleeced
Lutheran Holland, for tomorrow's feast.
The Netherlandish lengths, the Dutch heirlooms,
That might have graced my movements and my groom's,
Fade on the fat sea's bellies where they hung
Like cover-sluts. Flesh, wet linen wrung
Bone dry in a washerwoman's raw, red,
Twisting hands, bed-clothes off a lovers' bed,
Falls off the chains. At Valladolid
It fell, flesh crumpled like a coverlid.

Young Carlos de Sessa stripped was good
For a girl to look at and he spat like wood
Green from the orchards for the cooking pots.
Flames ravelled up his flesh into dry knots
And he cried at the King: *How can you stare*
On such agonies and not turn a hair?
The King was cool: *My friend, I'd drag the logs*
Out to the stake for my own son, let dogs
Get at his testes for his sins; auto-da-fés
Owe no paternity to evil ways.
Cabrera leans against the throne, guffaws
And jots down to the Court's applause
Yet another of the King's *bon mots.*
O yellow piddle in fresh fallen snow –
Dogs on the Guadarramas . . . dogs. Their souls
Splut through their pores like porridge holes.
They wear their skins like cast-offs. Their skin grows
Puckered round the knees like rumpled hose.

Doctor Ponce de la Fuente, you,
Whose gaudy, straw-stuffed effigy in lieu
Of members hacked up in the prison, burns
Here now, one sacking arm drops off, one turns
A stubble finger and your skull still croons
Lascivious catches and indecent tunes;
And croaks: *Ashes to ashes, dust to dust.*
Pray God be with you in your lust.
And God immediately is, but such a one
Whose skin stinks like a herring in the sun,
Huge from confinement in a filthy gaol,
Crushing the hooping on my farthingale.

O Holy Mother, Holy Mother, Ho-
ly Mother Church, whose melodious low
Labour-moans go through me as you bear
These pitch-stained children to the upper air,
Let them lie still tonight, no crowding smoke
Condensing back to men float in and poke
Their charcoaled fingers at our bed, and let
Me be his pleasure, though Philip sweat
At his rhythms and use those hateful tricks
They say he feels like after heretics.
O let the King be gentle and not loom
Like Torquemada in the torture room,
Those wiry Spanish hairs, these nuptial nights,
Crackling like lit tapers in his tights,
His seed like water spluttered off hot stone.
Maria, whose dark eyes very like my own
Shine on such consummations, Maria bless
My Philip just this once with gentleness.

The King's cool knuckles on my smoky hair!

Mare Mediterraneum, la mer, la mer
That almost got him in your gorge with sides

Of feastmeats, you must flush this scared bride's
Uterus with scouring salt. O cure and cool
The scorching birthmarks of his branding-tool.

Sweat chills my small breasts and limp hands.
They curled like foetuses, *maman*, and cried.
His crusted tunics crumple as he stands:
Come, Isabella, God is satisfied.

JOHN HAYNES

Stickman

The human body is the best picture of the human soul
Wittgenstein

I can be mortgaged to anything. It can be deducted at source
and I won't feel any loss. A wife calls me but it's not my name,
it's not me answering. I can never know myself.
A child draws me: I'm the charcoal figure without feet
growing up from the pavement, whose hands pass
into black cups and saucers. I can be any shape.
My love can be any action. I can be racked, wrenched,
bent arthritic. I can survive inside conditioned reflexes,
doctrines, mechanisms, bricks, officers of field rank,
trousers. Necessity's some such thing. My topology
doesn't alter: my head's got to be one end, my feet always
the other. I stay labile. *You ought to see me dance.*

PETER DALE

Unposted letter

A column-inch, all said.

If I'd had what you needed most
the day stopped in your head
You'd have got it in the post.

Not Laurie's but yours the death
and I could come and show
him frost gone at a breath,
frost-scaled cones,
the lawn of thaw-thrushed snow.
But you are grown too old now
to divert from the cold
tenter of tall bones.

There's nothing I could say
to comfort you, no hope
to hold out where you grope.
But let grief have its way.
I'll try to share – though son,
not father, and my breath
when all is said and done
would merely return, return
your wandering concern
to the day he took to death.

Cold what comfort I raise.
Listen to your own grief
heaving. No son's grave
yet dark shall draw his cries.
This and what safety he has
from the random cancer cell

or radio-active haze.
Don't talk of death for one
who never saw the skeleton
of a wren beyond the sill.

Yet all that I could say,
this constructed hope,
is the mere wish to help,
landscape ruins the sea
erodes. For your concern
I'd hack a mask of ice.
Your tears still gleam in the sun
and there is nothing else
I know to calm your pulse
or hide those chilling eyes.

The day's re-iterative tick
is the only sure relief
from anguish in this life –
or drugs. I know you'll take
time, though if I had
books or something to pass
the day stopped in your head,
I'd send them. Kinder a card
phrased in conventional code
and scrap this wordy piece . . .

Once in a crowded bar
above the give and take
of all the lunch-time talk,
feeding on cheap beer
and cheese sandwiches,
Peter just said: 'But now
only the pops and jazz
move me.'
  And all I spoke
the usual handy pack.
He was there – someone I knew.

Fire
and water
are the only dead that move.

Note: The poem was written on reading of the death of the son of an old family friend, recorded briefly in a national newspaper.

TOM RAWORTH

Going to the zoo

shapes that come in the night
three tulips through my window
hair brushed in the next room

the black panther extends his leg
here is the site of the battle of maldon
mum ee mum ee mum ee

the order is all things happening now
no way down through you float in the density
so sensitively turned on the animals

KEN SMITH

The pity

I cut my hands on the cords at the strangling post
but no blood spilled from my veins
instead of blood I watched and saw the pity run out of me
Mao tse-Tung

She was destroyed, and my child ceased in her belly.
In Kiang-si we had walked in the clear morning,
she hanging back, barefoot, childbig. Crossing
the plank bridge I saw the falling mountain
with its stream hang still. The land lay like a bowl
of pebbles, hills behind me at its rim. A hawk
splayed in the wind, dived to kill; so sparrows die.
China was patience you said: the sketched lines
of valley, of the reaching twig, all still, rest in motion;
a large pale flower twitching, a flower waiting, open.
So a vast land itched for death, its people mild
and ministered.

But the cockroach and the grinning toad
drawn beautiful was China; the fly grown fat on flesh,
glittering in heat. I was lashed and drained
of the gentle passion. Patience was prised from me.
I picked lice from my hair. You thought me gentle still.
I ate filth, wore it, would have died in filth.

The horned and hanging bat sees a bat's world.
Fish quiver in the shallows, cold as their element,
thinking water. I wore contempt, grew hatred.
I was locked and jailed. She that was my wife
was garotted. Compassion had not anything to do
with this: she was destroyed where I could hear,
and the child ceased in her.

Compassion cannot go forever in the sun,
paraded, bowing, twiglike. It rests,
and somewhere takes the hawk's wing, diving.
She was destroyed, and my child ceased.
I cut my hands on the cords at the strangling post,
but no blood spilled from my veins;
instead of blood I watched and saw the pity run out of me.

Family group

He also was a stormy day: a squat mountain man
smelling of sheep and the high pasture, stumping
through pinewoods, hunched and small, feeling
the weather on him. Work angled him.
Fingers were crooked with frost, stiffened.

Ploughing, he would fix his eye on the hawthorn,
walking firm booted, concerned for the furrow.
Horse and man in motion together, deliberate,
one foot put before the other, treading cut clay.
He would not see the bird perched on the plough.
He would not chase the plover limping over stubble.

He was my father who brought in wood and lit
the hissing lamp. And he would sit, quiet
as moor, before the fire. She drew him
slowly out of silence. She had a coat
made from a blanket and wore boy's shoes.
She was small and had red hands, firm boned,
and her hair was greying. The house was stone
and slate. It was her house, his home,
and their family; and they quarrelled often.

She churned butter, baked, and scrubbed floors,
and for twenty years he laboured the raw earth
and rough weather. In winter we made mats
from rags with pegs. We guarded ourselves,
and were close. We were poor, and poorer banking
each safe pound. Each year passed slowly.

Now he lives in the glass world of his shop,
and time is grudged. Ham and tinned meat
and vegetables are his breathing day.
He works harder and is unhappy. She too
stoops through the labouring year, is greyer,
and grumbles. Nothing is made any more
but money, that cannot be made. Nothing
means happiness. The light comes down wires,
water through tubes. All is expensive, paid.
Silence is gone from their lives; the city
has taken all that poised energy. Violence
is articulate. The deliberate motion is gone,
and he moves with pain through time that is work
that is cash. He will not notice the crashed
gull fallen in the storm, the grabbing sparrow.
She cannot ease him into speech, or be content
before the broody fire. She is in fashion now.
But seasons pass them without touching.
They will not feel the winter when it comes.

Leaving

Putting my head to you
I said Yes
a heart
beats
gently:

a child reaching
into its fingers'
quivering,
within you
an immense
small shiver
of silence
contained like a sound
in its bell.

I, who sit over a poem
trying to see what is
pressed into light
confess being moved
more by death:
a darkness almost
not possible;

I have felt even a stone
itch to unfold itself
and the sea's crying
in the shell of my skull

We create as the husks
of the grass
bear seed,
wanting like grass surely
to obliterate
earth's darkness.
The earth we have risen from
in a blind rearing
urges us,
the earth broods under us

I ask
tell me it is not this
a dark we go into
shut like a stone

The night boat

Wherever it stops it will dock, there will be land and an open harbour. It sails in, there are the sounds of water against the wooden keel, knockings, creakings of ropes, water lapping against itself. It is open day, the sunlight striking calm water, in the distance rain is forming itself in a dark head of cloud. Black sails, black wood, ebonies, and around them clouds, gullcries, brown weeds floating in the sea. On the boat and all round it it is night: a deep blackness in which the boat pitches, wherever it goes. There are ship-lights before and aft, a dimmer light shines through the boat's windows. On deck a door is thrown open, the light casting outward is yellow, ancient. Where it spends itself pass dark bent figures, darker shapes of the light who if you could hear them would be muttering *Aleppo*, *Tangiers*, *Malacca*, over and over. A seaman, sitting in the prow, guides the boat in to the quay; all that can be seen of him is the spark of his pipe that glows with his breathing, slow and even, the effort of an old man. When the boat is tied up they will roll the sails, they will open the holds and haul out their cargo, which is always darkness.

Eli's poem

I met a woman from the sea coast,
she took me aside in the bushes
and wrapped me around and said *we are alone*
as the moon up there is with just two sides.
I did what was to be done and came away with her

Now I am with a crazy woman
who hurts herself with ashes and briars
running in the scrub. She takes blankets
and stuffs them under her skirt for a child.
She takes out the blanket and croons on it,
washes it, beats it with sticks till it cries
and tears it to pieces. Her lament
goes down the street on cut feet in the gravel.
She runs in a nightgown thinking she's the police
and charges anyone with ridiculous crimes
like wearing a hat sideways and walking wrong.
The people here know her and smile and say
yes they will come to the court to answer.
She writes everything down in her book.
In bed she's like trying to catch a hare.
She wants to sleep with me all night
till my back breaks, if I doze off
she wakes me crying for love.

I married a crazy woman for her brown hair.
At first I thought she was pregnant
but her blood runs, the doctor shakes his head at me.
I tell her your child is in the other country
and will not come here because of your frenzy.
She runs to the church crying she's evil,
the priest holds out his god's battered arms
and says *come child everyone's evil.*
I cool her with my breath, I cool her with water.
She's insatiable as the river, like winds
she has no place to go and runs
from whatever does not move. She's holding a wooden
knife and staring it down till it becomes pure menace
and I fear it myself. I sleep with her
because then I control her and know where she is,
but I don't know what runs in her.
Now she is out on the hill wailing
cutting her flesh on the stiff grass
where I go to her lamenting

T. J. BRINDLEY

Joan's essay

A dirty wart weighed down
her crusted eye
which watered like a sore:

her mouth was welded, a harelip
clawed at her words
which yelped like vermin.

She knew all this. She wrote,
'I was born in a zoo.
When they seed me they all screamed.'

I gave six out of ten.
She looked through her watery screen
at my impertinence.

JOHN BARRELL

from *Some versions of pastoral*

3.

1332 6. 109 Huts partly clay & partly brick.
a little child in æ: gown of green – cow salting corn-distraction – Scare crow – oblong fields – mounds of earth – furze dead and living – poor hawthorn hedges – a wide road – wide spaces on each side of it barefoot Women. Women washing Linen basket in Eden
The *Notebooks* of S. T. Coleridge

From my cottage built of whatever does build a cottage
I came out wearing my frock which is always green;
The cows were chewing on salt and choked on their porridge
When I said to them, 'what does corn-distraction mean?'

A man with a notebook was coming along the turnpike,
And whatever you said to him he would write it down:
'Why, child, is your father's field so long and thin-like?'
'Why's yours so short?' I replied, with a hitch of my gown.

By the cottage door there's a heap of corn-distraction,
Which we use (as you know) to fertilize the ground:
This gent nosed around it and said that an excavation
Would show it was really an ancient burial mound.

'It isn't, but will be,' I said, 'and now if you please it's
Time I was cutting some furze and some scratchy briar,
We burn them, you know.' 'Ah, furze!' he said, 'like the phoenix
The furze is living and dead, not consumed by the fire –

'You'd do better to burn the hawthorn, then, though the hedges
Are poor here.' 'Poor!' I cried as I kicked off my shoes,
'There's nothing as poor as a girl in the lakeland villages –
For the price of a meal I could even be your Muse.'

But the other nymphs of the village were down by the Eden,
And heard all this as they stood barefoot in the stream.
What they did to the gent I'm sure *I* can't imagine,
But *he* could – for him a pipe was as good as a dream.

JEFFREY WAINWRIGHT

1815

1. The mill-girl

Above her face
Dead roach stare vertically
Out of the canal.
Water fills her ears,
Her nose, her open mouth.
Surfacing, her bloodless fingers
Nudge the drying gills.

The graves have not
A foot's width between them.
Apprentices, jiggers, spinners
Fill them straight from work,
Common as smoke.

Waterloo is all the rage;
Coal and iron and wool
Have supplied the English miracle.

2. Another part of the field

The dead on all sides –
The *fallen* –
The deep-chested rosy ploughboys
Swell out of their uniforms.

The apple trees,
That were dressed overall,
Lie stripped about their heads.

'*The French cavalry*
Came up very well my lord.'
'*Yes, And they went down*
Very well too.

Overturned like turtles.
Our muskets were obliged
To their white bellies.'

No flies on Wellington.
His spruce wit sits straight
In the saddle, jogging by.

3. The important man

Bothered by his wife
From a good dinner,
The lock-keeper goes down
To his ponderous water's edge
To steer in the new corpse.

A bargee, shouting to be let through,
stumps over the bulging lengths
Of his hatches,
Cursing the slowness
Of water.

The lock-keeper bends and pulls her out
With his bare hands.
Her white eyes, rolled upwards,
Just stare.

He is an important man now.
He turns to his charge:
The water flows uphill.

4. Death of the mill-owner

Shaking the black earth
From a root of potatoes,
The gardener walks
To the kitchen door.

The trees rattle
Their empty branches together.

Upstairs the old man
Is surprised.
His fat body clenches –
Mortified
At what is happening.

TOM PICKARD

'The devil's destroying angel exploded . . .'

no sound
but horns of southern ships
and flapping wings

no colour
but dancing black

producers of heat
confused in the cold

moon full above the dole

sleep children of chilled night
whose fathers were black men
(a miner's bright eye is no slave)

sleep bairns shiva now
ya fathas gold is stolen

strong fathers of a harsh past
despondent now
slagg faces rot against the dole

your hands held hammers
& demanded much
the moment passed
bairns curld cad in the womb

worried troops and churches –
you suffocated in the Durham Bishop's stables
when Londonderry's jails were full

the coal you hewed should have burnt
them alive

instead you begged another shilling

beneath jagged brows
    & stooped backs
making others rich
with the dust which killed you

you should have thrown it in their faces like a bomb
fed your children joyful stories
of the blood of those who
cheat us

where we live
shattered smiles
break on haggard faces

manufacturers of filth
marry our wealth in a confetti of votes

no breath of slum air

councillor elected by my father
he said you wore a workers cap
called everybody marra
but the word I heard was slave

bloodfluke in the brain of an ant
that gold chain was scraped
from the lungs of pit men

your gown is a union leader
gutted and reversed

look dozy fathers look
your masters have changed
drawn by the rivermist
you drift in a dream

ah father your flesh is overrun with lice
and all your life you nurtured many parasites

BARRY MACSWEENEY

Poem

we sit for weeks
in a tortoise-shell box,
holding hands to our faces
to collect tears; we receive stones.

we receive curious animals & stones.
the lovely reason leaves
town again, she goes, she
is, I'm sure, feminine. she goes
and she receives tears. gives us
stones.

Quaker meeting

It is wrong for the world ever to be a picture.
Not a model, not an image, it is the world:
when Rome falls it is Rome that falls, and graven
pillars are pillars lying along the world.

'A deer is shot with an arrow, not with what the arrow
means' – and my father so shook the church with his prayer
for steadiness that we all decided a long time ago
to follow dim trails on in the sand when the river ends.

Very reluctant we are to call us even a church,
where the stovepipe flakes real rust on oak pews
while our people mouth First-Day mistakes,
one at a time – wrong, wrong.

But as true in this world as the bell in our heads
can be, we seek our selves and hold communion,
silently.

The stranger

The place he wanted to tell about
lay beyond, lay far. It had
no name; it hardly differed from this,
but it was apart, and thus deserved
our thought. He spoke on.

There were bushes he wanted us
to see. And the rocks had a certain
subdued gleam when the sun came;
they were not precious, just different,
and other, and odd . . .

A mountain was there that
you could not see from here.
A stream just smaller than ours bent
and made a park where in winter
deer and elk spelled out their trails.

He spoke on. The world had
such special and lost places in it!
He shook his head when we offered
him a rest. No, no, he would be
getting along. Those bushes –
they had little berries, like salal,
to eat, but sour, but . . .

After he left I felt insignificant things:
leaf prints on my hands,
at my heels the tug of my shadow,
the hollow away off there, waiting –
towns where we almost lived.

JOHN BERRYMAN

To B— E—

O unimproveable.
My Tri-Regatta! My four-minute mile!
My *Antony & Cleopatra* thirsting & burning lust!
My mortal love.

O I was to the least ineffable impression
of a mere ghost of your thought
open, and I'll have it – I can afford it – cast in bronze.
Lesbia lives, past ages; and her admirer.

Too often, as too often you plained to me,
we did it.
'What do you think you are? a sexual athlete?'
You once sighed to me, after a pause: 'O yes!'

Ah, after those years; & later, stark
you lay back on my thick couch in Manhattan
& opened yourself & said 'Kiss me'.
I sucked your hairs.

O my grave love now, probably grey-haired
(horror) & even more (dear love) distinguished,
if you dropped your hand to me
I'd take the next plane to London.

The search

I wondered ever too what my fate would be,
women & after-fame become *quite* unavailable,
or at best unimportant. For a tooth-extraction
gassed once, by a Russian woman dentist in Detroit.

I dreamed a dream to end dreams, even my dreams:
I had died – no problem: but a mighty hand
was after my works too, feeling here & there,
& finding them, bit by bit.
At last he found the final of all one, & pulled *it* away, & said
'There!'

I began the historical study of the Gospel
indebted above all to Guignebert
& Goguel & McNeile
& Bultmann even & later Archbishop Carrington.

The Miracles were a stumbling-block;
until I read Karl Heim, trained in natural science;
until I had sufficiently attended to
The Transfiguration & The Ecstasy.

I was weak on the Fourth Gospel. I still am,
in places; I plan to amend that.
Wellisch on *Isaac & Oedipus*
supplements for me Kierkegaard.

Luther on *Galatians* (his grand joy)
I laid aside until I was older & wiser.
Bishop Andrewes' account of the Resurrection-appearances
in 1612 seemed to me, seems to me, absolutely it.

I studied Titian's remarks on The Tribute-Money.
Bishop Westcott's analysis (it took him 25 years)
of the first eighteen verses of *St John*
struck me as of a cunning like Odysseus'.

And other systems, high & primitive,
ancient & surviving, did I not neglect,
sky-gods & trickster-gods, gods impotent,
the malice & force of the dead.

When at twelve Einstein lost belief in God
he said to himself at once (as he put it later):
'Similarly motivated men, both of the past & of the present,
together with their achieved insights,
waren die unverlierbaren Freunde' – were the unloseable friends.

JOHN HAINES

The Middle Ages

Always on the point of falling asleep,
the figures of men and beasts.

Faces, deeply grained with dirt,
a soiled finger pointing inward.

Like Durer's Knight, always haunted
by two companions:

The Devil, with a face like a matted hog,
dishevelled and split;

and Death, half dog, half monkey,
a withered bishop with an hour-glass.

There's a cold lizard underfoot,
the lancehead glitters in its furry collar;

But it's too late now to storm the silence
on God's forbidden mountain.

You have to go on as the century darkens,
the reins still taut in that armoured fist.

The wreck

The Church, like a wreck blown ashore
from the Middle Ages,
battering on a shoal at Finisterre . . .

The seams have opened,
and the sea, like a luminous window
falling away, flashes briefly
with ikons, chalices, gold candlesticks.

Angels and saints, their faces
crusted with salt,
draw near to the flooded railing.
They try to sing – the wind,
full of a wintry fervour,
whips the kyries from broken spars.

And the figurehead on a cross
has never moved . . .

A couch mourns in the littered shallows;
unwieldy shapes, driftwood and sea-coal,
groan and struggle to their feet,
survivors from a shipwreck of souls.

The Goshawk

I will not walk on that road again,
it is like a story one hesitates to begin.

You find yourself alone,
the fur close about your face, your feet
soft and quiet in the frost . . .

Then, with a cold, rushing sound,
there's a shadow like the death-angel
with buffeting wings,
his talons gripping your shoulder,
the bright beak tearing and sinking . . .

Then, then you are falling, swept
into the deepening red sack of a voice:

Little rabbit, you are bleeding again;
with his old fire-born passion
the Goshawk feeds on your timid heart.

'It must all be done over . . .'

Wherever I look the houses are coming down,
the yards are deserted,
people have taken to tents and caravans,
like restless cattle breaking stride,
going off with their wagons
under a rumbling cloud.

I have begun to believe those rumours
of the world's wheat being eaten
by metallic grasshoppers,
and columns of brutal strangers
advancing on the soul of Asia.

I hope I shall be able to leave
without too much baggage
or bitterness. I must make my life
into an endless camp,
learn to build with air, water, and smoke . . .

JAMES WRIGHT

The poor washed up by Chicago winter

Well, I still have a train ticket valid.
I can get out.
The faces of unimaginably beautiful blind men
Glide among mountains.
What pinnacles should they gaze upon
Except the moon?
Eight miles down in the secret canyons and ranges
Of six o'clock, the poor
Are mountainously blind and invisible.
Do they die?
Where are they buried?
They fill the sea now.
When you glide in, poor men cast shadows
You can trace from an airplane.
Their shoulders are huge with the barnacles
That God has cast down into the deep places.
The Sixth Day remained evening, deepening further down,
Further and further down, into night, a wounded black angel
Forgotten by Genesis.
If only the undulations of the shadows would pause.
The sea can stand anything.
I can't.

I can remember the evening,
I can remember the morning.
I am too young
To die in the sea alone without
Any company.
I can either move into the McCormack Theological Seminary
And get a night's sleep,
Or else get hauled back to Minneapolis.

PHILIP LEVINE

They feed they lion

Out of burlap sacks, out of bearing butter,
Out of black beans and wet slate bread,
Out of the acids of rage, the candor of tar,
Out of creosote, gasoline, drive shafts, wooden dollies,
They Lion grow.
                    Out of the grey hills
Of industrial barns, out of rain, out of bus ride,
West Virginia to Kiss My Ass, out of buried aunties,
Mothers hardening like pounded stumps, out of stumps,
Out of the bones' need to sharpen and the muscles' to stretch,
They Lion grow.
                    Earth is eating trees, fence posts,
Gutted cars, earth is calling in her little ones,
'Come home, Come home!' From pig balls,
From the ferocity of pig driven to holiness,
From the furred ear and the full jowl come
The repose of the hung belly, from the purpose
They Lion grow.
                    From the sweet glues of the trotters
Come the sweet kinks of the fist, from the full flower
Of the hams the thorax of caves,
From 'Bow Down' come 'Rise Up,'
Come they Lion from the reeds of shovels,
The grained arm that pulls the hands,
They Lion grow.
                    From my five arms and all my hands,
From all my white sins forgiven, they feed,
From my car passing under the stars,
They Lion, from my children inherit,
From the oak turned to a wall, they Lion,
From they sack and they belly opened
And all that was hidden burning on the oil-stained earth
They feed they Lion and he comes.

A soldier of the republic

(To P.L., 1916–1937)

Gray earth peeping through snow,
you lay for three days
with one side of your face
frozen to the ground. They tied your cheek
with the red and black scarf
of the Anarchists, and bundled you
in canvas, and threw you away.
Before that an old country woman
of the Aragon, spitting on her thumb
rubbing it against her forefinger,
stole your black Wellingtons,
the gray hunting socks, and the long
slender knife you wore
in a little leather scabbard
riding your right hip. She honed it,
ran her finger down the blade, and laughed
though she had no meat to cut,
blessing your tight fists
that had fallen side by side
like frozen faces on your hard belly
that was becoming earth. (Years later
she saw the two faces
at table, and turned from the bread
and the steaming oily soup, turned
to the darkness of the open door,
and opened her eyes to darkness
so that they might be filled with anything
but those two faces squeezed
in the blue of the snow and snow and snow.)
She blessed your feet, still pink,
with hard yellow shields of skin
at heel and toe, and she laughed
scampering across the road, into
the goat field, and up the long hill,
the boots bundled in her skirts,

and the gray hunting socks, and the knife.
For seven weeks she wore the boots
stuffed with rags at toe and heel,
she thought she understood
why you lay down to rest
even in snow, and gave them to a nephew,
and the gray socks too.
The knife is still used, the black handle
almost white, the blade
worn thin since there is meat to cut.
Without laughter she is gone
ten years now,
and on the road to Huesca in spring
there is no one to look for you
among the wild jonquils, the curling
grasses at the road side,
and the blood red poppies, no one
to look on the farthest tip
of wind breathing down from the mountains
and shaking the stunted pines you hid among.

The sorrel filly

The songs of small birds fade away
into the bushes after sundown,
the air dry, sweet with goldenrod.
Beside the path, suddenly, bright asters
flare in the dusk. The aged voices
of a few crickets thread the silence.
It is a quiet I love, though my life
too often drives me through it deaf.
Busy with costs and losses, I waste
the time I have to be here – a time
blessed beyond my deserts, as I know,
if only I would keep aware. The leaves
rest in the air, perfectly still.
I would like them to rest in my mind
as still, as simply spaced. As I approach,
the sorrel filly looks up from her grazing,
poised there, light on the slope
as a young apple tree. A week ago
I took her away to sell, and failed
to get my price, and brought her home
again. Now in the quiet I stand
and look at her a long time, glad
to have recovered what is lost
in the exchange of something for money.

NATHAN WHITING

(from *Poems of an ownerless slave*)

Getting whipped

Standing in the room,
I,   very alone,
    am whipped all the same –
    as if i had owners.
I pull the curtains over my back,
Suddenly feeling blood filled,
    about to break.
    i want to look behind me –
I turn and turn and turn,
My eyes are unfocused.
    there is no one there.
    i'm being whipped by habit.

She

Held my hand
After i bought her.
    in the morning i saw
    the slaves doing their jobs.
For a night
I'd wanted her to own me.

National soil

In my dreams i escaped,
Ran into the night
    digging through the weeds
    to a peg nailed shack
    without a wall.
When i came in
The cat left

To climb a dead tree,
  to watch the men catch me,
  put me in jail.

Six wardens accuse me.
  i ask them,
  and they say i'm an american.
Oh please not that.
I'm a slave.
  but with a convict's suit?
  i must be an american.
I have a fever.
I want to bleed on the floor.
I try a while,
    i can't.
Oh hell
Americans are free.
  that's good,
  i should be happy.
Free in jail
Is better than being a slave.
 i walk around for a while.
No!
  but the bars start leaning
  and flapping in the wind
  like the old flag.

The judge comes up
  and says i can be a slave again
If i find an owner.
  i rip up those bars i'm so happy.
I woke with his hammer on my thumb.

In a line

  what holds us together
Marching in a line?
We don't own our shadows.
  they take no food

and do no work.
My shadow is a cheap slave
Paid to follow other shadows.
He is on the auction block
looking very proud
with me standing beside him.
A lot of shadows went that day
holding us together.

Cowbirds

are in the corn field
Because they have no other place
To spread their wings.
but why must they drink my tea
so impolitely
And steal my cloves?

They will fly around
And drop them on some
poor slave's child
living in his shack.
It's not like the spice islands
Believe me.

I'm illegal

as a slave.
Ever since Lincoln
They've been fighting modern wars
to prove it.

I've worn a trail
In trying to escape
to enemy lines.
Valor forgotten
No one would give a uniform.
finally a person gets lost,
Dust keeps falling on to

Your stolen helmets.
    then someone wins.
But they wouldn't
Geneva convention, population rehabilitation,
otherwise violated,
own me.

I've thought about
Being illegal.
    the laws
Aren't alone.
They have me to comfort them
    where they don't exist.

I started writing

Were this a memoir of my hands
I could complete it;
    but,
It is the middle of winter,
    february 8, 1967 –
    very cold.

Dear journal,
    i wrote my name a list,
I asked for help.
Only one guy wanted me,
    claims to have owned me all along.
It's a good feeling.

Happy today

Among an army of men,
Doing as i'm told,
    knowing no man
    has been the slave
    of a greater purchaser.
There's mud coming down
In the slave quarters –

everything is that color,
that texture.
It works against your hands,
But you're a slave.
sometimes the mud is so shiny
that you can see yourself in it
As you work, getting stuck more and more,
Seeing yourself in the mud.
i salute you mud,
you're better than chains.

MIROSLAV HOLUB

Oxidation

An invisible flame hovers over the tables.
Eager compounding of elements
of something with nothing,
of something that isn't said
with something that is,
a hidden endothermic mess.

The process goes on
in one ear
out of the other,
the brain grinds the poisoned corn
and behind the glass wall a big sewer-rat
swells like
the pink-faced patron of barbers;
gentle, continuous opening of the veins.

We grow, turning to ashes.

And into the wrinkles, monotype
of non-self on self
settle the oxides of silence
and the hydroxides of resignation.

Doesn't matter.

There won't be any gold. The philosopher's stone
is not in the plan.
Smoke from the copybooks and drawings falls into the mouth.
Not having words, we applaud.

And inside,
inside this retort of human skin
a huge ashen statue forms,
with tear-rimmed eyes
and white trembling lips
which at night when

roots dance and a star whistles
repeat the empty ashen primeval word
Later Later Later Later.

(*Ian Milner*)

School

Enter a tree, bowing and saying:
I am a tree.
A black tear drops from the sky and says:
I am a bird.
Here now, approaching
along a cobweb
comes something like love,
and it says:
I am silence.

But then there sprawls in front of the blackboard
a national democratic
horse in a waistcoat
and repeats,
pricking his ears to every side,
repeats and repeats:
I am the driving force of history
and
we all
love
progress
and
courage
and
the wrath of warriors.

And then from under the classroom door
trickles a thin stream
of blood.

For here begins
the quartering
of the innocent.

(*George Theiner*)

Discovery of fire

He went
and picked it up,
brought it
in a container
of silicon glass,
with asbestos gloves,
in the indifferent darkness.

He showed it to them,
the blue-purple
gay
flame,
deeply troubled
that it was not going to work,
that it was not it.

It was it,
the first steak
could be smelt
and the feet of the first heretic
started to burn.

Zeus didn't give a damn
and Hera
really liked it.

He, Prometheus,
returned
to think up
the blow-torch.
but it didn't work out this time

and only fetters
grew on his ankles
& wrists
& out of his grey head
flew an eagle
and jabbed
and jabbed.

(*Jarmila and Ian Milner*)

A Nazi air-raid warden

He rang our bell
and yelled:
Your blackout is faulty,
I can see a light!

We switched the light off
and sat in the dark.

A little later
he rang our bell
and yelled:
Your blackout is faulty,
I can see a light!

Man has his limits.

As he left
the street writhed
and dogs felt their hair standing on end,
for they knew that his word
had the power
to turn them
into lice
or into knights of the Holy Grail
with oak leaves and swords.

The world has its limits.

Even the dark can be switched off
for a time.

But then
not even that.

(*George Theiner*)

The heart

Officially the heart is
oval and muscular,
full of desire.

But if you've ever drawn a heart you know
that it is also

prickly like a star
and sometimes bedraggled
like a stray dog at night
and sometimes huge
like an archangel's drum.

And sometimes cubical
like a draughtsman's dream
and sometimes gaily rotund
like a ball in the net

and sometimes it's like a thin line
and sometimes like an explosion.

And in it there is
only a river,
a weir,
and at most a single fish,
and not a goldfish at that.

Rather a grey little
jealous
whiting.

This, of course, is not obvious
at first sight

If you've ever drawn a heart you know
that first you had to
take off your glasses,
push aside the mirror,

throw away your ballpoint
and carbon paper

and go out
for a long
stroll.

(*George Theiner*)

PAAVO HAAVIKKO

One thing at a time

(from *Leaves are Leaves*)

One thing at a time.
It is spring.

Autumn
Is autumn,
Nails
Are nails.
Spring passes, autumn passes, hair is gone,
It is spring.

Eyes were, three blind mice are,
Their nails oscillate, like they do when it's autumn,
It is spring.

Scientific thought presupposes,
That's as maybe,
Hair, nails, wife, children, these I have sent
So as not to generalize the discrete, away,
And there her nails grow and they grow
Nails long as night,
It is spring.

The fir-trees at play

(from *Flower Songs*)

The fir-trees at play,
Cones raining down
Ceaselessly,
O you, the wood cutter's
Daughter,

Steep as the mountains,
As gruff, and as gorgeous,
Listen,
If you never loved, if I
Never loved (your
Bitterest words
When we parted), O listen
To the cones, raining down upon you
Abundantly, ceaselessly,
Without mercy.

(*Anselm Hollo*)

MAILA PYLKKONEN

The flowers

As I am, possibly, going to die here
I tell you: leave me under the open sky,
cowering on the ground, like the Stone Age dead.
Let the frost break my bones,
snow cover, spring uproot my hair,
let the small caretakers of the forest arrive and the big birds.
They will seek out my bones, still tasting of pine
and the green of leaves, where once my hair was rooted.

Let the bone-crushing animals come,
the birch-tree shed its leaves once more:
they will have nothing to conceal. The earth is
beautiful. I have found rest.

Sometimes
when I am tired I cry out
– she was talking to herself,
no one but her in the mirror:
– I am strong. I am light, light.
I always used to laugh. I'm a black pond,
they are throwing stones in the pond.
There, they are laughing.
And, what is black
where are the stones?
I am all surfaces, I move,
the stones keep falling into the void,
only the circles are real.
The laughter spreads,
waking small echoes
dying away, returning, always
dying away. I smile. They
smile, at me. We all have

that we want.
The calmness of her face.
Her eyes, blue, close together;
the purple of almost invisible veins
on her cheekbones.
Sitting on the porch, discussing
her flowers. Dandelions,
she was old enough
to include them
in her garden. She said
what she had to say, always
that she was a widow
that cats don't like to swim
but when they do,
they go like this –
and a tunnel was built, for the railroad,
and she broke her leg, and the longboat
that overturned and sank, with all those people;
yes, and even cows
can be very strange creatures.
Then we counted her savings,
she kept in a handkerchief
tied with seven knots.

(*Anselm Hollo*)

PENTTI SAARIKOSKI

The madman's horse

I bought a horse from a madman.
He had drawn it himself
And it was a regular horse
But for the eyes: they were in its nostrils.
Still, that was
Intentional: that people would see
How mad he was, and buy more drawings.
I bought it. I thought of the horse,
Thought of it standing, among the pine-trees
In the evening, when the sun's ears
Are streaming with blood.

Making the sun run

1.

I'm in a fix.
Surrounded by these so
    socially useful
        Animals . . .
No matter what
I say or how.
I'm in worse than a fix.

2.

Light in a hostel window.
Someone moves in the room.
The houses' outlines dissolve in the fog.
    Not so much to see.

Says 82-year-old Asberg the engineer,
Still, so much to do! and now
my eyes begin to fail. He observes
the stars,
draws weather-charts.

3.

Fall mists like an old man's gestures
drift.
I walked the path that followed the curve of your smile.
Talked to men who died long ago.
This
was my work.

4.

Worst
the nights. His self-pity
dozing in daytime in the ceremonial
folds of megalomania and plans
wakes up:
the images block out sleep.
They swell to choke him
in the narrow room.
He would like to shatter himself, but instinct
decayed into vanity, holds him back
and his nostalgia-feelers vibrate
away, from what feeble touchings.
He fears
the little girl who makes the sun run
at her bidding.

5.

Sand tinkling, glass – or a revolution?
Sparse landscape, and
no talk.

Of the good times, the happy events
and comings together
little is held
in the mind.

Life was given to man

(from *Greek Sequence*)

Life was given to man
for him to consider
in which position
he wants to be dead:

Grey skies float by,
star-meadows hang

and the earth
comes into your mouth
like bread.

(*Anselm Hollo*)

BERTOLT BRECHT

Of all works

Of all works I prefer
Those used and worn.
Copper vessels with dents and with flattened rims
Knives and forks whose wooden handles
Many hands have grooved: such shapes
Seemed the noblest to me. So too the flagstones around
Old houses, trodden by many feet and ground down,
With clumps of grass in the cracks, these too
Are happy works.

Absorbed into the use of the many
Frequently changed, they improve their appearance, growing enjoyable
Because often enjoyed.
Even the remnants of broken sculptures
With lopped-off hands I love. They also
Lived with me. If they were dropped at least they must have been carried.
If men knocked them over they cannot have stood too high up.
Buildings half dilapidated
Revert to the look of buildings not yet completed
Generously designed: their fine proportions
Can already be guessed; yet they still make demands
On our understanding. At the same time
They have served already, indeed have been left behind. All this
Makes me glad.

E. P. L'élection de son sépulchre

The production of petrifactions
Is an arduous business and
Expensive. Whole towns
Must be reduced to rubble
And at times in vain –
If the fly or the fern
Was badly placed. Furthermore
The stone of our towns is not lasting
And even petrifactions
Can't be relied on to last.

And he did not compare

And he did not compare those
With others
Nor yet himself with
Another, but,
Threatened, prepared to transform
Himself quickly
Into unthreatenable dust. And
Everything
That happened later, he carried out like
Something agreed upon, as though fulfilling
A contract. And extinguished
Deep inside him
Were all desires.
He strictly forbade himself
Every movement.
His thought and feeling shrank
And vanished, like an
Empty page he evaded everything
Except description.

(*Michael Hamburger*)

PETER HUCHEL

The journey

One evening,
Late in November between flat lakes,
A man stepped from behind rain bushes.
We took a path
Through tall rushes,
The air brushed cool
Against my temples as if I were
Walking between the manes
Of two horses. They carried
In sacks of fog
My luggage lighter
Than the night wind over the reeds.

Not the trailsman
Who among dry river pebbles
Can find a pigeon
And running water,
But the weak one
With the festering shoulder led me
Where white smoke
Drifted along the ground
Into thickets
Of thistles hard as iron.

Under the constellation of Hercules

A village
No larger
Than the circle
The hawk draws
In the evening sky.

A wall,
Rawly hewn, scorched
With russet moss.
A bell's toll
Carries across the glittering water
The smoke
Of olives.
Fire,
Feeding on stalks
And wet leaves,
Woven with voices
You do not know.

Bent low into the night,
Into the icy harness,
Already Hercules is dragging
The chain harrow of the stars
Up the northern sky.

(*Henry Beissel*)

JOHANNES BOBROWSKI

The Duna

Duna, dawn
and the splendid wind
of the plains always about you.
The old town lies in the smoke.

Cold your banks. Bushes,
a green strip. Your swallows
swoop into
the light.

Weary
at noon
I have come,
I fall on the sand.
I will live from the breath
of the streams, drink
from the springs, the waters
of earth and night, from secret depths
under the grass.

I will live in the fire
of day, part the flames
to see you: in the climbing year
you walk with a heavy mouth,
dark – the gulls
and the waters flash,
screaming the sea receives you –
you go towards it.

In its shadow,
from the old deep
the old creatures
sigh to you.

(*Ruth and Matthew Mead*)

HANS MAGNUS ENZENSBERGER

Karl Heinrich Marx

gigantic grandfather
jehovah-bearded
on brown daguerrotypes
i see your face
in the snow-white aura
despotic   quarrelsome
and your papers in the linen press:
butcher's bills
inaugural addresses
warrants for your arrest

your massive body
i see in the 'wanted' book
gigantic traitor
displaced person
in tail coat and plastron
consumptive   sleepless
your gall-bladder scorched
by heavy cigars
salted gherkins laudanum
and liqueur

i see your house
in the rue d'alliance
dean street   grafton terrace
gigantic bourgeois
domestic tyrant
in worn-out slippers:
soot and 'economic shit'
usury 'as usual'
children's coffins
rumours of sordid affairs

no machine-gun
in your prophet's hand:
i see it calmly
in the british museum
under the green lamp
break up your own house
with terrible patience
gigantic founder
for the sake of other houses
in which you never woke up

gigantic zaddik
i see you betrayed
by your disciples:
only your enemies
remained what they were:
i see your face
on the last picture
of april eighty-two:
an iron mask:
the iron mask of freedom

(*Michael Hamburger*)

MIKLÓS RADNÓTI

Red shore ('Veresmart')

The road has grown silent, a crow
wobbles across it like a pregnant woman.
'Well crow, finally!' The road sighs.
It talks and babbles about its sorrow.

Wounded seeds listen in the ground.
The battlescarred landscape's eyelashes flicker –
it hasn't forgotten, although dusk
rocks it more and more gently now.

A small mine is hidden in a little hole.
It glitters angrily, it wants to explode, but
it's afraid. Cabbages stare
at it darkly and hold it down.

There at the foot of a young tree,
behind the sunflowers bent over by their wisdom,
a steel blue fog hangs across in straight lines –
thick barbed wire waiting for blood.

But at dawn, when dew weighs it down,
(its stem is a gentle fuse)
very carefully the golden blossom of the
squash creeps through the wire and opens.

And in time, the silence drizzles again.
Now and then, a stork stands on the edge of a trench.
Florian plows over the approach trenches
which are rabbit holes now.

And the workers come back.
Weavers spin again,
they dream about fine thread
until the crystals of dawn wake them.

And women bend down again and again,
a new world grows at their feet.

Vain little girls in dresses red as poppies
and boys, like little butting goats, make noise.

And, soaked in the bearded light of the stars,
the wise order of the world returns,
the order of animals and ears of corn,
the stern but still gentle service regulations.

17 January 1941

Roots

Power glides in the root,
drinking rain, living in the earth,
and the apple is white as snow.

From underneath it rises and breaks through
the soil and crawls along secretly.
Its arm is like a rope.

On the root's arm a worm sleeps
and a worm sticks to its leg.
The world is rotten with worms.

But the root goes on living below.
It is the branch, heavy with leaves,
that it lives for, not the world.

This is what it feeds and loves,
sending delicate tastes up to it,
sweet tastes out of the sky.

I am a root myself now,
living among worms.
This poem is written down there.

I was a flower. I became a root.
There is heavy black earth above me.
The workers on my life are done.
A saw wails over my head.

Lager Heideman, above Zagubica in the mountains
8 August 1944
(*Steven Polgar, Stephen Berg and S. J. Marks*)

NATAN ZACH

Giant

I am a giant,
and only I
am a giant. Whenever I
raise my head, stars
touch my head. Whenever I
do not raise, nobody
pays
any attention that
I do not
raise.

How is it that one star

How is it that
one star, alone,
dares. How does he dare;
for heaven's sake.
One star alone. I
would not dare. And I
am, as a matter
of fact, not alone.

Honi

And to sleep, for this?
Seventy.
Is it seventy, or seventy-two; seventy years?
I can't be sure.
The grass is that young.

Is it seventy?
Honi: old Honi. A whole
circle of life, almost,
in sleep.
Circle?
What circle? Where did I hear
talk, where mention of
a circle? Circle?

Hard to remember. Where did
I hear talk of
a circle? And
for that,
to sleep?

Note: An ancient legend relates that in years of drought Honi drew a circle around himself and vowed not to budge until rain fell. The grateful people nick-named him 'Honi the Circle-Maker'. According to another legend, Honi once slept for seventy years. When he awoke, not even his grandson could recognize him. The sages congregated in the House of Study did not believe his claim that he was Honi, and treated him disrespectfully. Honi's spirits fell. Begging God's mercy, he died.

Against parting

My tailor is against parting.
That's why, he
said, he's not going away;
he doesn't want to part
from his one daughter. He's definitely
against parting.
Once, he parted from his wife, and
she he
saw no more of (Auschwitz).
Parted
from his three sisters and
these he never
saw (Buchenwald).
He once parted from his mother (his father
died of a fine, and ripe age). Now
he's against parting.
In Berlin he

was my father's kith and kin. They passed
a good time in
that Berlin. The time's passed. Now
he'll never leave. He's
most definitely
(my father's died)
against parting.

A song for the wise lovers

A song for the wise
lovers, who love, wisely.
Their days in blessedness pass.
Even in death, they will not age,
nor ever part, but inhabit
together the one house.

A song for the wise lovers
on their bed, who do not speak.
With a hand they turn the light
off, together close their eyes
blessing each other.
While one is reading he'll
have on the bed-side light.
Their children's breathing is
heard by the clock and
by the midnight's wind.

A song for the wise
lovers, who have built themselves
a house, and locked its doors.
Bolt the shutters; outside, it is cold, and
a wind, and storm is expected. A guest
will not arrive on such a night;
and if he comes, don't admit him.
It's late; and only frost blows through the world. The poet,
also, out of distress, not abundance, sings. Remain
embraced.

(*Jon Silkin and the author*)

DAVID AVIDAN

*Kas buvo–tai nebus**

Two ex-Lithuanians, who remember
their mother-tongue even more vaguely
than they remember their mothers, meet
in a café on a cool clear evening, and exchange
memories. How do you say 'past' in Lithuanian? Indeed,
how do you say it? Very, very strange. Perhaps
in this pleasing area there is someone, within
two miles at most, who can
do something about this. But
it gets late and all those Lithuanians
who aren't dead will be hard asleep.

How do you say 'sleep' in Lithuanian?

* A Lithuanian proverb: 'What has happened will never happen again.'

(*translated by the author*)

GIUSEPPE UNGARETTI

Vigil

A whole night long
crouched close
to one of our men
butchered
with his clenched
mouth
grinning at the full moon
with the congestion
of his hands
thrust right
into my silence
I've written
letters filled with love

I have never been
so
coupled to life

Cima Quattro, 23 December 1915

Brothers

What regiment d'you belong to
brothers?

Word shaking
in the night

Leaf barely born

In the simmering air
involuntary revolt

of the man present at his
brittleness

Brothers

Mariano, 11 July 1916

(Jonathan Griffin)

Agony

To die like thirsting larks
against the mirage

Or like the quail
the sea once passed
in the first bushes
because it has lost
the will to fly

But not to live on lament
a blinded finch

Another night

In this dark
with hands
frozen
I make out
my face

I see myself
abandoned in the infinite

Stars

Above us once again the fables burn.

They will fall with the leaves at the first wind.

But come another breath,
A new scintillation will return.

Quiet

The grapes have ripened and the field is tilled,

The mountain stands out from clouds.

On the dusty mirrors of summer
The shadow has fallen.

Between uncertain fingers
Their light is clear,
And far.

With the swallows flees
The final torment.

(*Charles Tomlinson*)

LEON FELIPE CAMINO

And for what have I come?

Ah yes!
I have come to see the bird in the cage
and the judge pressing onward with his gavel
those who build gates,
those who build padlocks,
those who build wire fences,
and those who fix green glass in the high part of thick walls.

But I have also come to see those who weave cables and long ropes.
Those who break rosaries and splice them afterward one with another so that the prayers will not bite their own tails . . .
and those who build canals
and those who build ladders
and those who cast sound lines in the shadows like spiders,
deep and thin sound lines
made with a carnal metaphysical and bitter secretion
which to understand in some way
men, for now, call tears.

(*Peter Glusker*)

CÉSAR VALLEJO

(from *Trilce*)

56.

Every day I rise blindly
to work to live: and I have breakfast
not tasting a drop of it, every morning.
Not knowing if I have made it, or ever shall,
something that leaps out from the taste
or is only heart, something come back that will lament
until this is the least thing here.

Children would grow up sated with happiness
                    oh bright morning,
before the sorrow of our parents unable to leave us unable
to escape their dreams of love for this world;
like God so full with love
they thought themselves creators
loved us with warm injury.

Ornate edges of invisible weft
teeth that hunt with a ferret from a blind of neuter emotions
                    columns
of no base no coronation,
in the huge speechlost mouth.

Match after match in the dark,
tear after tear in a cloud of dust.

57.

The highest points are cratered, the points
of the love of being the first letter, I drink, I fast, I sho-
ot heroine into the grief, straight
into the lank throb and against all correction.

Can I say they have betrayed us? No.
That they were all good? No again. But
a willingness exists there, without doubt,
and above all, that's how it is.

And what if you love yourself very much! I search for me
in my own design which ought to have been my own
work, in vain: nothing gained by being innocent.

All the same, who is pushing me.
To the point I don't dare close the fifth window.
And the act of loving the self and persisting, up against
the hours and the wrongness.

The man is Everywhere.

60.

Of wood is my patience,
silent vegetable.

Day, you have been pure, a child, useless,
born naked, the leagues
of your path, go running along
your twelve extremities, this grimbrowed folding
which later comes apart
into it isn't known what final infancies.

Constellated from hemispheres of clot
under eternal unknown americas, your great plumage,
you dispatch yourself and leave me, without your ambiguous
emotion
without your tangle of dreams, Sunday.

And my patience becomes worm eaten
and I turn to speak out: when will
come mute Sunday opening in the tomb,
when come to load up this Saturday
of rags, this horrible suture
of the pleasure which begets us unwillingly,
and the pleasure which IsoLates us.

(*Gordon Brotherston and Ed Dorn*)

ANTONIO CISNEROS

From a mother again

My sons & the rest of the dead still
belong to the owner of the horses
& the owner of the lands, & the battles.

A few apple trees grow among their bones
& the tough gorse. That's how they fertilize
this dark tilled land.
That's how they serve the owner
of war, hunger & the horses.

Paracas

Since early morning
the water has been rising between the red backs
of the shells

& fragile-footed gulls
chewing the small tidal animals

until they're swollen like boats
spread out beneath the sun.

Only rags
& skulls of the dead tell us

that beneath these sands
our ancestors were buried in droves.

Loneliness II

'Friend, I'm reading your old poems on the north terrace.
The oil lamp flickers.
How sad to be lettered & a clerk.
I'm reading about the free & flexible rice fields. I raise my eyes
& can only see
the official books, the expenses of the province, the yellowed
accounts
of the Empire.'

It was last summer & that night he reached my hotel on
Sommerard Street
I'd been waiting for him two years.
I hardly remember anything of our conversation.
He was in love with an Arab girl & that war
– the Fox Dayan's – was even more painful to him.
'Sartre is old & doesn't know what he's doing,' he told me &
also said
that Italy had made him happy with its empty beaches, sea
urchins & green water
full of fat glistening bodies, 'Like the baths at Barranco,'
a summerhouse built at the turn of the century & a dish of crabs.

He'd stopped smoking. And literature was no longer his trade.
The oil lamp flickered four times.
Silence grew strong as an ox.
And so to salvage something I told him about my room & my
neighbours in London
about the Scotswoman who'd been a spy in both wars,
about the doorman, & a pop singer
& having nothing more to tell him, I damned the English &
shut up.

The oil lamp flickered again
& then his words shone brighter than some beetle's back
& he spoke of the Great March, the Blue River with its turgid
waters
about the Yellow River & its cold currents & we imagined
toughening ourselves by running & jumping along the seashore

doing without music or wine, relying
for wisdom on our eyes only,
& none of this seemed like a mirage in the desert.
But my gods are weak & I doubted.
And the young stallions were lost behind walls
& he did not return that night to the hotel on Sommerard Street.
Obstinate & slow gods, trained to gnaw at my liver every
morning.
Their faces're dark, ignorant of revelation.
'Friend, I'm on the island that's going under north of the Channel
& I'm reading your poems,
the rice fields are full of the dead
& the oil lamp flickers.'

On the death of the Bishop, who was truly of your ilk

Lord, your accomplice
the bishop is dead.
Some old women
are weeping
among muted bells
& his debtors
observe joyful
mourning.
Lord, he was truly
your friend,
& at the business table
you worried
about his deals.
In the old days
you stuffed your chests
with Abel's things.
I also suspect
you knowingly
sent Jesus
to the slaughter-house.
(*Maureen Ahern and David Tipton*)

TADEUSZ RÓŻEWICZ

Draft for a contemporary love-poem

For surely whiteness
is best described through greyness
bird through stone
sunflowers
in December

in the past love-poems
described flesh
described this and that
eye-lashes for instance

surely redness
should be described
through greyness sun through rain
poppies in November
lips at night

the most telling
description of bread
is one of hunger
it includes
the damp porous centre
the warm interior
sunflowers at night
breasts belly thighs of Cybele

a spring-like
transparent description
of water
is the description of thirst
ashes
desert
it conjures up a mirage
clouds and trees enter
the mirror

Hunger deprivation
absence
of flesh
is the description of love
the contemporary love-poem

summer 1963

(*Adam Czerniawski*)

ZBIGNIEW HERBERT

A parable about Russian émigrés

It was in '20
or maybe '21
the Russian émigrés
appeared in our midst

very tall and fair
with romantic eyes
and dreamlike women

when they crossed the marketplace
we said 'wandering birds'

they went to county balls
everyone whispered 'what pearls'

but after the lights were dimmed
the helpless people were left

grey newspapers were stubbornly silent
but the game of patience showed mercy

guitars outside windows fell silent
even black eyes grew pale

a whistling samovar in the evening
carried them to familiar stations

after some years
only three were still mentioned
the one who went mad
the one who hanged himself
and she who had calls from men

the others lived quietly
and slowly turned to dust

This parable is told by Nicholas
who understands historical necessity
in order to frighten me that is convince me

The Captain's spy-glass

I bought it from a street vendor in Naples. He claimed it had belonged to the captain of the schooner *Mary* which one sunny day sank in mysterious circumstances off the Gold Coast.

A strange object. Whichever way you turn it, all you see are two blue bands: one deep sapphire, the other sky-blue.

(*Adam Czerniawski*)

GUNNAR EKELÖF

Xoanon

In you I possess a miracle-working Icon,
If to possess is to possess nothing:
As she possesses me, so I possess her.
She was given to me on the day she appeared
At a time and place decided upon beforehand,
And the same Panayía is revealed
Whenever the heart so wishes. Supported by her arm,
On a footstool in receding perspective,
Stands a grown-up baby in gorgeous swaddling-clothes
Who is the last Prince of my line.
I remove him, for everything that pertains
To this Panayía is removable,
As a robber can wrench
The silver-smith's basmá from some image
With smoke-blackened hands and worn away by kisses.
I remove the crown, I remove the two angels,
The annunciators of bliss
From the clouds and the gold ground in the upper corners;
I unfasten the jewelled clasp of the Maphorion
And remove the veil from the hair and the neck;
I relax the creases over the right breast,
And the creases over the left
Gently, to ease the pain. I remove like a spider's web
The thin slip that leaves the riddle
Both solved and unsolved, and she looks at me,
The eyes brown in the bluish-white of the eyeballs,
Steadfastly look at me. I remove the arms,
The brown hand with its rose, and the brown breasts,
The right breast first, then the left, but gently
To ease the pain, then the scalp and cheeks,
And the girdle after having kissed it,
And lastly the big eyes which look at me,
Steadfastly look at me still

After they have been removed.
I remove the gold ground and the ground coat
Until the thick-veined wood is exposed,
A piece of old olive wood, sawed long ago
Out of a storm-felled tree
On some coast way up in the north. In the wood,
Almost hidden, an eye, the eye-knot of a twig
That must have been broken off when the tree was still young
You look at me. Hodigítria. Philoúsa.

(*W. H. Auden and Leif Sjöberg*)

Notes:
Xoanon: Ancient wooden statue in Greek temples, i.e. an icon
Basmá: Print, printed goods, esp. printed cotton hangings
Maphorion: Head-dress, veil
Hodigítria: The woman who leads on icons
Philoúsa: The one who loves (or kisses); a type of madonna on icons

A world in each human being

Each human creature is a world that's peopled
by blind inhabitants in dark rebellion
against the I set over them as king.
In every soul a thousand souls are prisoned
in every world a thousand worlds are hidden
and these blind worlds, these lower worlds are real
and living, though they never come to birth,
real as the I is real. And we the kings
we princes of the possible within us
we too are subjects, prisoners ourselves
in some great being whose essential I
we grasp as little as our master can
his master. And our own emotions
have taken colour from their love and dying.
As when far out a liner passes, under
the horizon, lying smooth and clear
in the evening light. And we know nothing of it

until a wave swells towards us on the beach,
first one, and then another, and then more
that break and climb and break till everything
is as it was again. Yet nothing
is as it was again.

And so we shadows shake with strange unrest
when something tells us that a voyage has started,
that something of the possible is freed.

(*Ann Draycon*)

Byzantium

With these beings I have everything in common
They bind me with no bonds
With these beings I have nothing in common
They bind me with no bonds.

To these beings I am not obliged
and they have no demands of me:
I am a guest of the place's genius
but I can move my tent of potter's clay

Now they are bringing forward their low table, their sophrá
their small feast
of dewdrops, nectar, honey baked with seedflour
O the sweet Turkish cakes, sweet crushed against sweet
the tiny snowballs powdered with pounded sugar
loukoúmi, that pink-grey paste, sweet spiced against sweet
and over the whole a sprinkling of perfume
I watch them sit themselves down, preceded by proto-dervishes,
blinded fools, former emperors
followed by retinues, swarmed round by blind singers
with quavering larynxes.
They clamour, they lean against one another
They raise their goblets, hurl them without a sound at one another
under the cobwebs' baldaquins and serpentines
in hairy, gay or grotesque masks in strange

ankle-length costume – 'Is tin Polin! Is tin Polin!'
And now they are taking away their low table.
The meadow stands untouched outside the plexiglass window
No one has stepped on its glistening
I have never gone that way
There are no footmarks in the grass.
Only Athene, radiant-eyed, approaches
sober, dangerous, compelling
The moment of night is over

(*David McDuff*)

Someone said: I saw a dancing man

Someone said:
'I saw a dancing man
on the beach of a green dream
with the swell that wandered in under the surface
In the sunset the dancer shone red
He powdered his body with ground bones
mixed with the purple-red of spices
and splintered shavings of brick
What does it mean that he danced on the beach
surrounded by those who blindly saw in the sun?'
It means he was dead
or would shortly die.

And you who have once seen such a strange man dancing
you yourselves will never dance again
be it in love, in hope or in despair
You are long since dead, all of you, and vanished.

(*David McDuff*)

NAZIM HIKMET

Letters to Taranta-Babu

1.

Her father's twenty-fifth daughter
and my third wife
my eyes, my lips, my everything
                    Taranta-Babu
I send you
            this letter from Rome
without including anything with it
                    but my heart.
Don't be cross with me
because in this city of cities
I have failed to find
            a better present
                    than my heart.

Taranta-Babu
this is my tenth night here,
and now I sit
            my head bent on gilded books
which tell me stories
                of the birth
                    of Rome.
And there! . . . The lean she-wolf
                    and behind her
plump and naked Romulus and Remus
walk about my room.
Oh, but do not weep;
this Romulus
            isn't the same man
as that blue-beads merchant signor Romulus
who
    in broad daylight
in the market place of Wal-Wal
raped your fig-bosomed sister.

This one is the first Roman, King Romulus.
Whenever he roared towards the open sea
from the slopes of Antium
waves would knock each other down
and beat the shores of far Corsica
And whenever he raised his hands
towards the sky
he would grip the thunders by their long hair
and thrust them on to the ground.
. . . As if his father was the boxer, Carnera
and his mother Il Duce Mussolini.

Romulus and Remus
the twins of Silvia,
grandchildren of Venus . . .
Ignoring
their
tears
one dark night
she left them there.
Neither
a festoon of bayleaves
round their heads
nor decent pants about their loins.
In those days, Taranta-Babu,
our land Ethiopia
was not conquered
painted green colonial;
Banco di Roma had not been established.
So, Romulus and Remus
one early morning
thought to themselves:
'What the hell
can we do
around here?'
Then they went and met a female wolf,
they killed her cubs
they had their fill of her milk
and then sauntered along
and founded

this city, Rome.
They did, but
Rome became too small
for the two of them.
Thus, one evening
blaming his brother
for jumping over the dividing wall
Romulus wrang off his brother Remus' head.

That's what's said, Taranta-Babu,
in these gilded books:
In the foundations of Rome
exist
bucketfuls of milk of a she-wolf
and a palmful of blood of a brother.

2.

Three strings of necklace
made from the teeth of a blue monkey
round your neck;
living like a red-feathered bird
under the sky
or running like a stream on this earth –
your words mine
your eyes mine
reflecting me,
mother to my third daughter
mother to my fifth son
Taranta-Babu!
For months now
I have knocked on every door
street by street
house by house
step by step
in the middle of Rome
I searched for Rome.
No more
do the great masters

cut the marble like a silk fabric;
no wind blows from Florence;
no poems from Dante Alighieri
nor the embroidered face of Beatrice
nor the kissable hand of Leonardo da Vinci.
Michelangelo
                    is a fettered slave in museums
and from his jaundiced neck Raphael
                    is hanging on a cathedral wall.
In these days,
            in the long, wide avenues of Rome
there's only one dark
                        one blood-stained shadow,
leaning against the concrete banks
erect like a fasces,
chopping off
                    a slave's head
                            at every step,
at every step
                    desecrating a grave,
                                passing –
this shadow is Caesar.
Roma
'*Quo vadis Roma?*'
do not ask.
Just like in our own land
                    the same sun drenches the land here. . .
But shush, Taranta-Babu
with love
                    and respect,
smiling
            laughing,
shush!
And listen:
in the suburbs of Rome
the sound of the breaking chains
                            of Spartacus.

3.

Taranta-Babu,
today I have seen
Pius XI, the Pope.
Just as we have, in our tribe,
a Great Magician,
here, they have him.
But,
the difference is:
our Magician doesn't get paid
for banishing a blue devil
with three heads
to the Harar Mountains;
wild mares for sacrifice
and two loads of ivory a year
cover his debts.
But this holy Pope
cannot hope
the same from wild mares.
This dear gentleman
employs ambassadors in black robes
embroidered with gold crosses;
employs soldiers in short drawers, gay gaiters –
they look at his hand
he looks at theirs.

One of the free citizens of this beautiful Italy,
a woman
who sells her lips with corporate excitement
and lies on her back for half an hour for half a lira,
buys a small picture of this holy man
for half of that money,
hangs it above her bed
seeking forgiveness for her sins.

I looked at him:
neither a Saint George
nor a Saint Peter,

neither of them had gold-rimmed spectacles
but only uncombed
                    long
                              oily beards.
Pius XI, Taranta-Babu, like a shepherd
with a herd of soft-furred, black sheep
is grazing spirits in the grassland
            of crowned and uncrowned kings.
Pius XI
        who is
                the Ambassador of One
        born in a manger without a father
in order to be nearer to Virgin Mary
torments his body,
                    and every night
sleeps in a palace with marble columns.

4.

Suns in each embroidered design on silk shawls;
the hoof-sound of black mules towards Pompeii;
Verdi's heart beating
                in the colourful box of a barrel-organ;
and the best macaroni in the world . . .
like these, Taranta-Babu,
Italy is famous for her fascism, too.

Bolting through the lands
                of the great Counts of Emilia
and through the steel safes
                of Roman bankers
this fascism has come and hit the bald head
                of Il Duce
                as if it were a light,

A light,
        Taranta-Babu,
which will soon descend
on the graves
in the fields
of Ethiopia.

5.

To see
to hear
to feel
to think
to speak
to run without stopping,
to run
oh, to run
Taranta-Babu
heeeeey
to hell with it all
what a beautiful
thing
it is to be alive!

Think of me
while my arms embrace your wide hips
mother to my three children,
think warmly,
think of the sound of a naked drop of water
dropping on a black stone.
Think of the colour
the flesh, the name of the fruit
you like most,
think of its taste in your eyes
of the red red sun,
pure green grass
and of the huge blue blue ray
blossoming forth from the moon.
Think Taranta-Babu:
man's
heart
mind
and arm
have pulled from the seventh depth
of the Earth
and shaped so many fire-eyed, steel gods

who now can perish the world
                    with a single blow;
the pomegranate that fruits one in one year
          can fruit one thousand;
and the world is so large
so beautiful
               and the shores so infinite
that at night we can lie on the sand
               and hear the starred water.
How wonderful it is to be alive
                    Taranta-Babu
               how wonderful Life is!

To understand it as a masterpiece
to hear it as a song of love
and to live like a child wondering,
to live
          one by one
               but all together
as if weaving the most wonderful silk cloth.

Ah, to live . . .
But how odd, Taranta-Babu,
nowadays
'this incredibly beautiful activity'
this most joyful feel of all things
has become
so difficult
so narrow
so bloody
          undignified.

6.

(This part is chiefly in prose; it is suggested (i.e. in the 1965 ed. of *Taranta-Babu*, Istanbul, by the editor Şerif Hulûsi) that several allusions in this 'letter' refer to some Turkish men of letters of the '30s who had tried to malign Hikmet; some of them were successful. These characters have been bitterly satirized by Hikmet in his collection *Portreler* (Portraits), 1935.—*Translator's note.*)

7.

I know well
that no more than six questions
stand on the shelves of your mind
like a line of corked bottles . . .
You are as desperately illiterate
as a legal authority!

But even then
supposing I ask you:
'what would you do
if
our goats lost their long curly hair;
if the milk that ran
like the two arms of light
from their two-teat udders
suddenly stopped;
if the oranges of our country
began to dry on branches
like baby suns;
and if famine started to walk
on its skeleton legs
as if it were the native king of our soil –
What would you do?'

You will say to me,
'I myself will start to fade away
losing my colour drop by drop
as a starry night
that fades
with the first rays of the sun –
what a thing to ask an African woman
like me?
For us famine is certain death;
plenty, endless joy.'

What wisdom is this, Taranta-Babu,
here in Italy it is the reverse.

People die in time of plenty:
people live when famine comes.
In the outskirts of Rome
men walk like sick, hungry wolves;
but the granaries are bolted, locked
although the granaries are full of grain!
The looms can weave such silk cloth
                    enough to cover the way
                              from here to the sun,
but people walk without shoes,
                              people are in rags.
WHAT a bewildering world!
While the fish are drinking coffee in Brazil
babies go without milk here . . .
They feed people with words,
the pigs with choice potatoes.

8.

Mussolini talks too much, Taranta-Babu,
on his own
                    without friends
                              like a child
thrown into the dark night.
Shouting
                    and waking up at his own voice
kindled with fear
                         and burning with fear,
unceasingly prating!
He is talking too much, Taranta-Babu,
because
                    he is sore afraid.

9.

(At the beginning of this letter there is a picture of a wireless set – *Note in the original.*)

Something came to my mind today –
                    a picture

without lines
without words, Taranta-Babu.
And suddenly
I longed to see
not your face
not your eyes
but your *voice*, Taranta-Babu
cool like the Blue Nile,
deep like the wounded eye of a tiger,
your voice.

(Here in the letter there is a cutting from a newspaper which reads:

'MARCONI IL DUCE'S FAITHFUL PRIVATE

It is reported that Marconi has told a group of journalists today that he is at the command of his leader Mussolini. After successful tests, it is rumoured that Marconi's new invention, some kind of deathray will soon be tried out in Ethiopia. . . . This ray')

is his
who has freed voices
into the sky
like birds with blue wings;
his hands have picked
the most beautiful songs
like ripe fruit from the sky –
but now
the slave of the black-shirted Benito
he's about to stain his hands up to the elbow
with the blood of my brothers.
Upon the Ethiopian soil, it seems
that Count Marconi
the share-holder
the multi-millionaire
at the Banco Commerciale
will murder the great Scientist Marconi.

10.

(At the beginning of this letter also there is a newspaper cutting which reads: 'Italian forces are waiting for the end of the rainy season and the coming of the Spring before they start their attack on Ethiopia' – *Note in the original.*)

How strange, Taranta-Babu,
in order to kill us on our own soil
they're waiting for our own Spring
                    to blossom.

How strange Taranta-Babu!
This year in Africa
the end of the rain,
                    the coming
of all colours and scents
like a melody from the skies –
the stretching moist soil under the sun
like a bronze-skinned woman from Galla –
they'll all bring us death
                    at the same time
                    as your sweet bosom's awakening.

How strange, Taranta-Babu,
that death
                    shall walk in through our door
tucking a Spring flower
                    in his colonial hat.

11.

Tonight
Il Duce
on a grey horse
at the aerodrome
gave a speech
                to 500 pilots.
Finished it.
Tomorrow
                they'll be flying to Africa.

But he, himself,
is now eating spaghetti Bolognaise
at his huge palace.

12.

They're coming Taranta-Babu,
they're coming to kill you,
to pierce your tum
to see your intestines
on the sand
wriggle like hungry serpents.
They're coming to kill you, Taranta-Babu,
to kill you
and your goats, together.
Yet, you don't know them
and they don't know you;
neither have your goats jumped
over their garden fences.

They're coming, Taranta-Babu,
some from Naples
some from Tirol
some torn away from a loving gaze
or from a soft
warm hand
some of them.
As an army
as a battalion
as a squadron
but soldier by soldier
the ships have brought them
crossing three vast seas
to death,
as if to a wedding ceremony.
They're coming, Taranta-Babu,
from the heart of a conflagration;
and once they have flown the flag
from the sunbaked roof

of your earthen house
they may all go back –
but even then
the lathe turner from Torino
who's left his right arm in Somalia
will no longer work with his steel rods
as if working with bales of silk-thread.
And the fisherman from Sicily
will no longer see the light of the sea
through his blinded eyes.

They are coming Taranta-Babu,
and these men who come to die and to kill
will soon tie tin crosses
on their bloody bandages
the moment they return home.
Then,
in the great and just city of Rome,
shares will go up, banks will flourish
and our new masters will replace the soldiers
to rob the dead.

Last letter

(In this prose letter the young Ethiopian informs his wife Taranta-Babu that he may be shot by Mussolini's agents. He encloses a number of press cuttings. Hikmet might well have taken the information contained in these from contemporary papers for the benefit of his invented Ethiopian. But to check their authenticity would be an impossible undertaking because Hikmet does not quote dates though he gives the names of the Italian papers. The following letter is the last 'poem'; it consists of statistics which Hikmet must assiduously have put together in order to demonstrate under what conditions the Italians were, at that time, fighting a war against the Abyssinians. – *Translator's note.*)

WAGES IN ITALY

If we were to take the wages of an English worker as a unit of 100, then:

America	120
Canada	100
England	100
Ireland	80
Netherlands	72
Poland	50
Spain	30
Italy	29

Unemployment and Bankruptcies in Italy

	U	B
1929	300,786	1,204
1930	425,437	1,297
1931	731,437	1,786
1932	932,291	1,820

These statistics, Taranta-Babu, comprise the balance-sheet of Italian fascism. What will happen in the years to come? The answer is with the young soldiers who have come to die on our soil.

(*Taner Baybars*) (1935)

Sunday

Today it is Sunday.

Today, for the first time,
they have let me go out in the sun,
and for the first time in my life
I have looked steadfastly at the sky,
astonished
that it should be so distant,
so vast,
so blue.

I am sitting on the ground
filled with respect,
my back pressed to a white wall.
There's no question now
of plunging among the waves.
No struggle,
no liberty, no wife.
Earth, sun and myself;
I am a happy man.

(*Iain White, from the French*)

ALEXANDER BLOK

The Twelve

1.

Black evening.
White snow.
Wind! Wind!
Careful, man, or down you go.
Wind ... wind ...
Roaring the wide world over!

The white snow eddies
The white snow hisses
On sheets of murderous ice.
People slither
And slip on the ice ...
Watch out there! Oh, poor fellow!

From window to window
A cable stretched
With a streamer attached:
'All power to the Constituent Assembly!'
Grannie stares with frightened eyes,
Can't imagine what it signifies.
'What's it doing up there,
That silly old rag of a placard?
Think of the knickers the kiddies could wear,
And them going round half-naked ...'

Grandma, henwise, flaps and flutters
Over to the snow-drift's yonder side.
'Mother of Christ, preserve us!
The Bolshies'll murder us all in bed!'

A wind that flays!
The frost, if anything, worse!
And the bourgeois at the crossways
Digs his frozen nose in fur.

But who might this be? Long, lank hair,
And muttering at the vacant air:
'Traitors! Traitors!
Woe to Russia!'
Must be a writer or a
Soap-box orator . . .

Beyond the snow-drift, on his own,
Stands one with priestly garb on . . .
Wherefore now so woebegone,
Comrade parson?

Remember how majestically
Belly-first you'd pace,
With the cross upon your belly
Beaming at the populace?

The lady in the astrakhan
Walks up, accosts another:
'We sobbed as only lovers can . . .'
Slip, *slither*, and
Flop – she's over!

Easy, easy,
Ups-a-daisy!

The wind is merry
And vicious and gay;
He mows pedestrians
Over like hay;
Rips, wrenches, and yanks
The great streamer away:
'All power to the Constituent Assembly!'

And snatches on his way:

'So we organized a meeting
Here inside this building . . .
Held a discussion
Passed a resolution:
Ten for a moment, twenty for the night . . .
And not one kopek under that . . .
Fair enough? All right . . .'

Late evening.
Empty street.
Beggar shuffling
Ill-shod feet
And the wind screaming . . .

'Lonesome, dearie?
On your ownsome?
Come to bed!'

Bread!
What's ahead?
Pass by!

A black, black sky.

Rage, rage, bitter rage
Seething in the heart . . .
Black rage, holy rage . . .

Comrade, be on
Your guard!

2.

The wind runs wild, the snowflakes beat.
Twelve men go marching down the street.
Black rifle-slings on shoulders gleaming;
Fires all round them flaming, flaming . . .
Fags a-dangle, caps askew –
You'd think they were a convict crew!
Liberty! Liberty!
We
Ain't
Got no cross!

Rat-tat-tat!

It's chilly, comrades, it's chilly!

'Johnny's in a pub with Katie . . .'
'Government roubles in her garter . . .'

'In the money, like I told you!
Once our Johnny, now a soldier!'
'Hey Johnny, son-of-a-bourgeois-bitch, you
Kiss *my* girl and see what hits you!'
Liberty! Liberty!
We
Ain't
Got no cross!
Johnny's having fun with Kate.
What can Kate be playing at?
Rat-tat-tat!

Fires all round them flaming, flaming . . .
Rifle-slings on shoulders gleaming . . .
Keep in step with the Bolshevik army!
Warily watches the merciless enemy!
Comrade, have courage! Keep hold of your rifle!
Let's give Holy Russia a bloody good bellyful!
Stolid old
Solid old
Fat-arsed
Russia!

She
Ain't
Got no cross!

3.

So the lads all went and hied them
For to join the gallant Reds
For to join the gallant Reds
For to lose their gallant heads!

Sweet life, you are so bitter,
So bitter-sweet you are!
Greatcoat torn and tattered
And a rifle made in Austria!

Bourgeois, bourgeois, you beware
When we set the world on fire
World on fire with flames of blood –
    Grant us thy blessing, O Lord!

4.

Snowflakes fly, the coachman cries,
Johnny and Katie go spanking by –
Swank electric battery-lamp
    Bobbing on the cab-shafts . . .
    Mind your backs!

In an army greatcoat, Johnny,
With his stupid physiognomy,
Twirls and twirls his black mustachios,
    Twirls and twiddles
    And jokes and fiddles . . .

Good old Johnny – ain't he tough!
Good old Johnny – can't he bluff!
    Holding Katie in his arms,
    Trying out his charms . . .

Head flung back in sheer delight,
Pretty teeth all pearly white . . .
    Oh, Katie, Katie, darling Katie,
    Little snub-nose Katie . . .

5.

Just below your neckline, Katie,
There's a knife-slash, newly scarred.
Just below your bosom, Katie,
Skin and flesh are sorely marred!

    Hey, hey, dance away!
    Come and see that ankle-play!

Frilly undies, fair and fetching –
Fetch away, then, fetch away!

For the officers a-letching –
Letch away, then, letch away!

Hey, hey, letch away!
Kill your conscience for a day!

Katie, have you clean forgotten
Him that hadn't time to bolt
From my knife? Or does your rotten
Memory need a little jolt?

Hey, hey, jolt away
Through the night till break of day!

Pretty clothes, it was, and chocolates,
Swish cadets and Army swanks . . .
Now it's pride of all the privates
And the darling of the ranks!

Hey, hey, sin away!
Sin'll keep you young and gay!

6.

The driver comes galloping back again,
And shouts, and roars, and hollers amain . . .

Stop, stop, there! Andy, lend a hand!
Quick, Peter! Get them from behind!

Rat-tararat-tat-tat-tat-tat!
The snow spits upwards in their tracks!

The cab – with Johnny inside – is bolting.
Let's try another! Ram your bolt in!

Rat-tararat! I'll make you smart
For pinching someone else's tart!

So dodge me, would you? Well, don't worry,
I'll settle up with you tomorrow!

But what of Katie? Dead, stone dead!
Shot right through the bleeding head!

Well, Katie, happy? Not a word . . .
Then lie there on the snow, you turd! . . .

Keep in step with the Bolshevik army!
Warily watches the merciless enemy!

7.

So the Twelve, with rifles shouldered,
Carry on into the night:
Only one – the hapless murderer –
Ghastly pale, as if in fright.

Faster, faster, and still faster
Urges he his hurried pace:
Round his neck a woollen muffler,
Horror written on his face.

'Why so glum and gloomy, comrade?
Why so miserable, mate?
Why so dismal and downhearted?
Conscience-stricken over Kate?'

'Once I loved that woman, comrades,
Till I thought my heart would bust . . .
Used to spend in her embraces
Nights of passion, nights of lust . . .

'All because there was a love-spark
In those laughing eyes of hers,
All because there was a birth-mark
On the shoulder that I kissed,
Like a fool, I pulled the trigger, went stark
Mad and shot her . . . Christ!'

'Well, of all the blinking blether!
Here's a proper rigmarole!
Must we hang around for ever
While you vivisect your soul?
Now then, pull yourself together!
Try a bit of self-control!

'This is not the time to spend in
Mothering the likes of you!
There's much bigger things impending;
We've got trouble coming too!'

Peter slows his pace a little . . .
Not in such a frantic hurry . . .

Seems to brighten up a little . . .
Now he's looking almost merry . . .

    Hey, hey!
Fun will drive your cares away!

Lock yourselves inside your flats!
Looters lurking in the streets!

Open every basement door!
Welcome in the starving poor!

8.

Sweet life, you are so deadly,
  So deadly dull you are,
    So full of nausea!

I'll sit on a fence and watch a bit
  Watch a bit
    Watch a bit . . .

Ruffle me hair and scratch a bit
  Scratch a bit
    Scratch a bit . . .

Crack a few nuts and munch a bit
  Munch a bit
    Munch a bit . . .

Pull out me dagger and slash a bit
  Slash a bit
    Slash a bit . . .

Fly away, bourgeois, fly away home!
    I'll drink a blood-and-water
    To the landlord's dark-eyed daughter
    For the evening when I caught her ...

Lord, spare the soul of this thine handmaiden ...
    Nausea!

9.

No sound of life throughout the city.
The Nevsky tower is strangely quiet.
There's no policemen left on duty –
Come on, let's have a real old riot!

The bourgeois stands there at the cross-roads,
And digs his frozen nose in fur;
While at his feet, with tail tucked under,
Cringes a mangy mongrel cur.

The bourgeois stands there, as if hungry,
Just stands there like a question mark;
The old world, like a starving mongrel,
Cowers at his feet, too cold to bark.

10.

    Now the blizzard's really blowing;
        Blizzard, hoy! Blizzard, hey!
    Can't see where your mates are going
        Half-a-dozen feet away!

Whirling in a white maëlstrom ...
Soaring skyward in a column ...
'What a snowstorm! Jesu mercy!'

'Peter, don't be such a sissy!
Did your holy bag of tricks
Save you from a fine old fix?
Superstitious bleeder, aren't you!

Use your ruddy common, can't you!
Who's got hands as red as red?
Who shot little Katie dead?'
'Bolshevik march wherever you go!
Warily watches the merciless foe!'

Onward, onward, you masses,
Working classes!

11.

... So the Twelve go marching on,
Unsanctified, unblessed ...
Grim and ruthless, every man
Ready for the worst ...

Steely-glinting rifle-barrels
Levelled at the unseen foe ...
Into empty streets and alleys
Where alone the storm-winds blow ...
Plunging knee-deep and regardless
Through the boot-ensnaring snow ...

Red flag flying
Right ahead.

Sound of marching's
Measured tread.

Foeman watching ...
Keep your head!

And the blizzard in their faces
Never ceases
Night or day.

Onward, you masses,
Working classes!

12.

... Onward still the Twelve go striding ...
'Something's moving! Who goes there?'
Nothing but the red flag riding
Through the snowflake-flurried air ...

Right in front – a freezing snow-drift ...
'Something's moving! Who goes there?'
Nothing but a starving mongrel
Cringing slyly in the rear ...

'Scat, you tyke, or else I'll stick your
Belly with my bayonet blade!
Old World, hop it – else I'll prick your
Filthy mangy mongrel hide! ...'

Snarling like a wolf that's hungry,
Tail tucked under; won't stay clear;
Shivering mongrel, homeless mongrel ...
'Answer, will you! Who goes there?'

'Who's that with the red flag flying?'
'Try and spot him if you can!'
'Who's that dodging round the buildings
Like a convict on the run?'

'I'll get hold of you, don't worry!
Whether you give up or not!
You'll be for it, comrade! Hurry!
Come on out, or else be shot!'

Bang! And nothing but the echo
Rings across from house to house ...
Nothing but the muffled laughter
Of the storm-wind in the snows ...

Rat-tat-tat!
Rat-tat-tat!

... Onward still the Twelve go striding;
In their rear – a starving cur;
And with bloody banner leading,

Hidden by the howling storm,
Safe from human hurt or harm,
Gently stepping through the blizzard,
With a pearly mantle covered,
White-rose crown upon his head –
JESUS CHRIST, THE SON OF GOD.

January, 1918
(Alex Miller)

MARINA TSVETAYEVA

Insomnia

6.

Tonight – I am alone in the night,
  a homeless and sleepless nun!
Tonight I hold all the keys to this
  the only capital city

and lack of sleep guides me on my path.
  – You are so lovely, my dusky Kremlin!
Tonight I put my lips to the breast
  of the whole round and warring earth.

Now I feel hair – like fur – standing on end:
  the stifling wind blows straight into my soul.
Tonight I feel compassion for everyone,
  those who are pitied, along with those who are kissed.

7.

In the pine-tree, tenderly tenderly,
  finely finely: something hissed.
It is a child with black
  eyes that I see in my sleep.

From the fair pine-trees hot
  resin drips, and in this
splendid night there is
  a ratchet going over my heart.

Homesickness

Homesickness!   that long
exposed weariness!
it's all the same to me now

where I am   altogether lonely

or what stones I wander over
home with a shopping bag to
a house that is no more   mine
than a hospital or a barracks

It's all the same to me, captive
lion   what faces I move through
bristling, or what human crowd will
cast me out   as it must

into myself, into my separate internal
world, a Kamchatka bear without ice.
Where I fail to fit in (and I'm not trying) or
where I'm humiliated   it's all the same.

And I won't be seduced by the thought of
my native language, its milky call.
How can it matter   in what tongue I
am misunderstood by whoever I meet

(or by what readers, swallowing
newsprint, squeezing for gossip?)
They all belong to the twentieth
century, and   I am before time,

stunned, like a log left
behind from an avenue of trees.
People are all the same to me,   everything
is the same, and it may be the most

indifferent of all, are those
signs and tokens which once were
native   but the dates have been
rubbed out: the soul was born somewhere.

For my country has taken so little care
of me that even the sharpest spy could
go over my whole spirit and would
detect no native stain there.

Houses are alien, churches are empty
everything   is the same:

But if by the side of the path one
particular bush rises
                    the rowanberry . . .

An attempt at jealousy

How is your life with the other one,
  simpler, isn't it?   One stroke of the oar
then a long coastline, and soon
  even the memory of me

will be a floating island
  (in the sky, not on the waters):
spirits, spirits, you will be
  sisters, and never lovers.

How is your life with an ordinary
  woman?   without godhead?
Now that your sovereign has
  been deposed (and you have stepped down).

How is your life?   Are you fussing?
  flinching?   How   do you get up?
The tax of deathless vulgarity
  can you cope with it, poor man?

'Scenes and hysterics – I've had
  enough!   I'll rent my own house.'
How is your life with the other one
  now, you that I chose for my own?

More to your taste, more delicious
  is it, your food?   Don't moan if you sicken.
How is your life with an *image*
  you, who walked on Sinai?

How is your life with a stranger
  from this world?   Can you (be frank)
love her?   Or do you   feel shame
  like Zeus' reins on your forehead?

How is your life? Are you
  healthy? How do you   sing?
How do you deal with the pain
  of an undying conscience, poor man?

How is your life with a piece of market
  stuff, at a steep price.
After Carrara marble,
  how is your life with the dust of

plaster now? (God was hewn from
  stone, but he is smashed to bits.)
How do you live with one of a
  thousand women,   after Lilith?

Sated with newness, are you?
  Now you are grown cold to magic,
how is your life with an
  earthly woman, without a sixth

sense? Tell me: are you happy?
  Not? In a shallow pit? How is
your life, my love? is it as
  hard as mine with another man?

(*Elaine Feinstein*)

VLADIMIR SOLOUKHIN

Berry

In the green woodland grass, three steps from the track,
A berry grew, and ripened to redness.
Now is the time to pick it . . . but there are plenty of berries in
 the wood,
I didn't come for this . . . three steps . . . and then bending
 down.
Let it go on hanging. When the rain splashes it,
 it will knock it to the ground,
Or a bird will peck it.
But the berry says to me:
'Don't be lazy, come over here, bend down you spoilt darling!
You are dull to the moment.
Pick me
And
Have some pleasure.
It is true I'm small. But the scents of the summer wood,
The sun's morning beam, the drop of rain fallen on the earth,
All are inside me, all are mingled there.
Put me in your mouth. Press me tenderly on your tongue.
Filter my coolness through your teeth.
Proceeding, glancing indifferently at the sun,
How many berries are there still in front of you?
They say that when you are dying you recall all the past,
What you have seen, where you have been,
 when you have been right or wrong.
Among other things,
Obscuring or pushing them aside,
Perhaps I shall be remembered, shall nod from the earth's grass.
Perhaps, remembering me, bright-red, with a white speck,
Just before the final descent of darkness,
You won't regret that somewhere you did not do something,
But that on this day
You didn't pick me.'

The willow

Of all the trees in our village,
The willow
Beyond the potato field
Had no luck –
They made a rubbish dump there.

Well, in the first place, it's not known whose she was,
Or who planted her there, and why –
We don't know.
If around other
Quite domestic and quite seemly willows,
It is always well swept and clean, as in a hut,
By that ill-conceived one
There's a pile of god-knows-what.
People bring scrap iron,
Galoshes, boots,
Quite useless now, of course,
(If they were good for anything at all they wouldn't bring them)
And when the cat dies, they dump it by the tree.
So encircled is the poor willow
With torn rags and rotting cats
That it is better now to give her a wide berth.

But still, when May comes,
Up to her knees in muck
She suddenly begins to gild herself peacefully.
She doesn't care a rap about the ripped galoshes,
The jars and tins and rags of clothes.
She flowers, as all her earthly sisters
Flower –
With a modest flowering,
With the purest, most innocent of flowers
Opening primordially to the sun.
And it shines. And everything smells of honey.
It happens that bees fly to her
In spite of the refuse at her base,

Bear away the flowers' translucent honey
To people who abuse trees.

(*Daniel Weissbort*)

ANDREI VOZNESENSKY

Goya

I am Goya!
The enemy flew like ravens over my appalling
        field: picked out my eye sockets.
I am sorrow.

I am war's own

voice, I am cities fired in the storms of
nineteen-forty-
one.

I am hunger-horror.

I am also the throttled
neck of the old woman hanged in the naked square, her body
        like a bell rocking –

I am Goya!

O grapes of wrath! I
        have driven on the West, have launched my volleys –
                I am the ash of the uninvited guest!
And I have hammered in hard stars like coffin-
nails on the memorial sky.

I,
Goya.

The first ice

In the telephone box the girl freezes,
her face is smeared with running tears
and lipstick, she huddles, peers

out from her chilly collar, aches –
blows upon her thin little paws –
icicle fingers! Earrings flash.
Back – alone as she is, along
the long, lonely, icy lane.
The first ice. The first time, it was,
first ice crackling in phoned phrases –
the frozen track shines on her cheeks –
first ice on her insulted ears.

Earth

We love walking
barefoot on the earth,
on the yielding, misty, homely earth.
But where? In Ethiopia?
Perhaps in Messina?
In the desert? In Havana?
In a village in Ryazan?
We are men.
We love walking about the earth.

Currents of the earth stream through us like a shudder.
Yet we are insulated from it, under
a shield of asphalt, cobblestones, cars . . .
We forget the smell of earth in our city affairs.
But suddenly we smile – at a green sapling
that bursts through city granite
like a geyser
springing! . . .

An earth in dreams appeared to me, without trenches and chains,
without detonation of mines: a dream of telescopes,
of lime-trees, eucalyptus, peacock rain-
bows, lifts on crazy ropes
and showers of aluminium!
A world of seas, of trains, of women –
a world all puffing and

fructifying,
marvellous as man! . . .

Somewhere on Mars he goes, a visitor from Earth.
He walks. He smiles. He takes out a handful of earth –
a tiny handful of that burning,
half-bitter, homely,
far-whirling,
heart-catching earth!

Parabolic ballad

Our destinies fly like rockets, in parabolas,
occasionally along a rainbow but more often in the shadows.

Who was that fiery redhead painter – Gauguin?
You can't keep a bohemian in a business programme.
To land in the royal Louvre, starting from Montmartre,
he had to
describe
an arc through Java and Sumatra –
just took off, leaving behind him the lunacy of money,
the clucking of matrons, the fetid academy,
took off and cancelled
terrestrial gravity.
Beery shamans sniggered over their glasses: 'The
plumb-line's shorter, the parabola's steeper,
copying the heavenly tabernacles'd be better!'
But he left them there, he roared up like a rocket
through a blast that snatched their ear-flaps and coat-pockets,
and he dropped into the Louvre – not the tourist-door Louvre
but an angry
paraboloid
crash through the roof!

Well, truth-seeking's as unpredictable as diabolo.
Maggots make for cracks – man has his parabola.

I knew a girl once, she lived quite near,
we studied together, sat tests. But see
where I got to! –
                                        was it on the wings of demons I
reached those reeling equivocal luminaries of Tbilisi?
Forgive me for such a jesterish parabola.
Dear shoulders, frozen, in a shadowy passageway . . .
O how you rang out in the gloom of the Universe
like an antenna-rod, so vibrant and tense!
I fly on still,
                              called to my terrestrial
touchdown by your clear-cold earthly signal.
How hard it is for us to take that parabola! –

But pronouncement and prognosis and paragraph are
swept aside by art, by love, by history

tracing their parabolic trajectory!
Galoshes flounder through a Siberian thaw . . .
Can the plumb-line be a short-cut after all?

(*Edwin Morgan*)

YEVGENY YEVTUSHENKO

Stalin's heirs

Voiceless that marble.
  Voicelessly the glass flashed.
Voiceless the sentry stood
  in the wind like a man of bronze.
But a ghost of smoke left the coffin.
  A breath squeezed through the cracks
when they carried it out by the Mausoleum doors.
Slowly the coffin hovered,
  its edges grazed the bayonets.
It too was voiceless –
  it too! –
    but voicelessly loud with dread:
inside, a man was
  blackly clenching his embalmed fists,
pressing himself to the cracks,
  pretending to be dead.
He wanted to be able to remember them all,
  all his burial party:
young boys from Ryazan and Kursk,
  rustic recruits:
in order that some day, somehow
  he would gather strength for a sortie
and rise out of the earth
  and fall on them, the rustic dolts.
He's thought up something.
  He's only refreshing himself with a nap.
And I make this appeal now
  to our government, I make this prayer:
to double
  and treble
    the guard at Stalin's slab,
that Stalin may never rise,
  or the past rise with him there.

When I say 'past' do you think I mean
what is most heroic or treasured,
Turksib,
Magnitka,
the flag over Berlin?
No, my meaning is
of a different past, measured
by denunciations,
by arrests of the innocent,
by neglect of the good of men.
We sowed seed honestly.
We honestly made metal pour
and honestly marched and
stood in ranks and were soldierly.
Yet he was afraid of us.
He believed in a great end but ignored
that the means
must be worthy
of the majesty of the goal.
He was farsighted.
Schooled in the laws of the struggle,
he littered the globe with the heirs of his throne.
It looks to me
as if the coffin has a telephone:
the Enver Hoxhas
still receive Stalin's instructions.
How far does the cable from this coffin stretch even yet?
No: Stalin hasn't given in. There are ways
of dealing with death, he reckons.
Out of the Mausoleum surely it was
him
we fetched?
But how are we to fetch
the Stalin out of Stalin's successors?
Some of his heirs trim roses in retirement,
yet secretly trust
such retirement is temporary.
Some too
are first at the microphone abusing Stalin but

these are the ones
  who when night comes
    yearn after the old story.
You can see how today
  it's hardly by chance that the heirs
of Stalin go down with thromboses.
  To them, who were once his props,
the days when the labour camps
  are empty are disasters,
the times when halls overflow
  for the reading of poetry are a blot.
The Party has told me
  I shall not cease
    from mental fight.
If someone repeats, 'The fight
  is over!' – I have no skill
    to bury my disquiet.
So long as Stalin's heirs go
  walking in the light,
I'll feel him,
  Stalin, in the Mausoleum yet.

(*Edwin Morgan*)

JOSEPH BRODSKY

The Jewish cemetery near Leningrad

The Jewish cemetery near Leningrad.
A circle of rotten plywood fencing
and behind it, lying in rows,
lawyers, merchants, musicians, revolutionaries.

They sang for themselves.
They accumulated money for themselves.
They died for others.
But in the first place they paid their taxes,
  and respected the law,
and in this hopelessly material world,
they interpreted the Talmud,
  remaining idealists.

Perhaps they saw more.
Perhaps they believed blindly.
But they taught their children to be patient
and to stick to things.
And they did not plant any seeds.
  They never planted seeds.
They simply lay themselves down
in the cold earth, like grain.
And they fell asleep forever.
And after, they were covered with earth,
candles were lit for them,
and on the Day of Atonement
hungry old men with piping voices,
gasping with cold, wailed about peace.
And they got it.
  As dissolution of matter.

Remembering nothing.
Forgetting nothing.

Behind the circle of rotting plywood fencing,
four miles from the tramway terminus.

(*Daniel Weissbort*)

BIOGRAPHICAL NOTES

DANNIE ABSE. Born 1923 in South Wales, educated Cardiff and London. Became interested in poetry during the Spanish Civil War. Recipient of the Charles Henry Foyle Award, 1960. He has published six books of verse, of which the last two are *A Small Desperation* (1968) and *Selected Poems* (1970). A new volume, *Funland and other Poems*, is to be published in 1973.

DAVID AVIDAN. Born 1934 in Tel-Aviv. There are nine books of verse in Hebrew, and one, translated by the author, in English: *Megaovertone Selected Poems* (1966). A slightly different version of the poem reprinted here appears in *Megaovertone* on p. 53.

JOHN BARRELL. Born 1943, is married and lives on the Essex coast. Teaches at the University of Essex. Has published a pamphlet of poems – *Property* (1966).

WENDELL BERRY. Was born (1934) and educated in Kentucky. Has taught at the University of Kentucky since 1964. Recipient of a Guggenheim Fellowship 1961–2. Has published four books of verse, of which the most recent is *Farming: A Hand Book* (1971).

JOHN BERRYMAN. Born 1914 in Oklahoma. Awards and prizes are numerous; most recent is the National Book Award, 1969. *Love and Fame* (1972) is the last of his ten books of verse. Died 1972.

ALEXANDER BLOK. Accepted as the foremost of the Russian symbolist poets. Blok's earlier lyrical work is, in the main, an exploration of personal relationships. 'The Twelve' (and 'The Scythians') are political poems in that they are concerned, 'The Twelve' especially, with the emergence of the new proletarian state. Blok's poem is not the work of a man facilely transferring his talent from a 'personal' to a 'public' mode. The political poems are as 'felt' as the so-called 'personal' poetry. The interested reader may compare Alex Miller's translation with those of, say, Yarmolinsky, C. M. Bowra, Jon Stallworthy and Robin Fulton. A critical biography of Blok is at present being prepared by Avril Pyman. Blok, who remained in the Soviet Union, was born in 1880 and died in 1921.

JOHANNES BOBROWSKI. Considered to be one of East Germany's finest poets, he established a European reputation prior to his death. A selection of his poems – *Shadow Land*, translated by Ruth and Matthew Mead – was published by Donald Carroll in 1966 and reprinted by Penguin Books in 1971. Bobrowski was born in 1917 and died in 1965.

BERTOLT BRECHT. Known it would seem more for his plays than for his verse, yet Brecht valued his poetry, and the small but useful selection translated into English and presently available is read eagerly. Michael Hamburger writes appreciatively of Brecht's verse in *The Truth of Poetry* (1970). Brecht was born in Germany in 1898 and died in East Germany in 1956.

TERRY BRINDLEY. Born in 1939 in Tyldesley (near Manchester), has written a play about Arkwright which was performed at Matlock in 1971. He took a degree at the University of Leeds and now lives and teaches in Derbyshire.

JOSEPH BRODSKY. Born 1940 of Jewish parents in Leningrad. A disciple of Akhmatova. In February 1964 he was condemned to five years' corrective labour on a state farm near Archangel for the crime of parasitism. He is now at liberty. In June 1972 Brodsky left the Soviet Union. A selection of his poems in translation appeared in 1967 under the title *Elegy for John Donne*, and a new selection is under preparation for Penguin Modern European Poets.

ALAN BROWNJOHN. Born 1931 in London, educated London and Oxford. Currently teaches at a College of Education in London. He has published four books of verse, of which the most recent is *Sandgrains on a Tray* (1969). A selection of his poems is included in Penguin Modern Poets 14.

LEON FELIPE CAMINO. Born 1884 in Spain. Was a cultural attaché in Panama shortly before the Spanish Civil War in 1936. He became an exile in 1938 and now lives in Mexico. For further work by Camino see Stanley Burnshaw's *The Poem Itself* (1965).

ANTONIO CISNEROS. Born 1942, Lima, Peru. Has published four books, of which the last two are *Comentarios reales* and *Canto ceremonial contra un oso hormiguero* (Havana 1968). For this last he won the poetry prize, sponsored by Casa de Las Americas, for the whole of Latin

America. A selection of his poems, translated by David Tipton, is to be found in *Peru: The New Poetry* (1970).

PETER DALE. Born 1938 in Surrey and educated there and at Oxford. He now lives and teaches in Surrey. There are three collections of verse, the latest of which is *Mortal Fire* (1970).

GUNNAR EKELÖF. Born Stockholm, 1907. He studied music in Paris and then took up oriental studies in London and Uppsala. As well as his own fifteen books of verse, Ekelöf translated many foreign poets into Swedish, including Eliot, Joyce, Auden, Baudelaire and Rimbaud. He died of cancer in 1968.

HANS MAGNUS ENZENSBERGER. Born 1929 in Bavaria, and grew up in Nazi Nuremberg. Has been on the staff of the South-West Regional Radio (while living in Norway) and then until 1961 worked in Germany as a publisher's reader. His poetry is socially and politically orientated, and avoids the rhetoric that such a commitment can entail. A selection of his poetry, translated by Michael Hamburger and Jerome Rothenburg, appeared in 1968 and was reprinted in Penguin Modern European Poets.

ROY FISHER. Born 1930 in Birmingham, where he was educated. Pianist with jazz groups from 1946; teaches in the Department of American Studies at Keele University. Four principal books of poetry and prose, of which the two most recent are *Matrix* (1971) and *The Cut Pages* (1971).

PAAVO HAAVIKKO. Born 1931 in Finland. Poet, playwright and novelist, his work has been translated into several European languages. His *Selected Poems*, translated by Anselm Hollo, appeared in 1968 and will be published in Penguin Modern European Poets.

JOHN HAINES. Born in 1924 Virginia, and educated at continental schools, in the United States and in the Hawaiian Islands. In the US Navy during the Second World War. Moved to Alaska in 1947, where he obtained a homestead. Awarded Guggenheim Fellowship 1965–6. National Council of the Arts Grant 1967–8. Since 1970 has been living in California. There are two books of verse: *Winter News* (1966) and *The Stone Harp* (1971).

MICHAEL HAMBURGER. Born in Berlin in 1924. Educated Edinburgh, London and Oxford. In the army 1943–7 and has travelled extensively. Apart from his university posts he has lectured principally in Germany and the United States. Bollingen Foundation Fellowship 1959–61. Has done a considerable amount of critical work, including *Reason and Energy* (1957) and *The Truth of Poetry* (1970); also translation, particularly *Hölderlin: Poems and Fragments* (1966) and *Selected Poems* of Enzensberger (1968). He has published seven collections of verse, of which the most recent is *Travelling* (1969). A selection of his poems is included in Penguin Modern Poets 14.

TONY HARRISON. Born in Leeds 1937 and took a degree in classics at Leeds University. He worked in Ahmadu Bello University in Nigeria 1962–6 and taught at Charles University, Prague, 1966–7. Held the Northern Arts Poetry Fellowship at Newcastle and Durham 1967–8. His book of verse, *The Loiners* (London Magazine Editions, 1970), was awarded the Geoffrey Faber Memorial Prize 1972. Harrison edited *Stand* for a year, and in 1968 produced the Czech issue of the magazine (vol. 10, no. 2). He has recently completed a new verse version of *Le Misanthrope* for the National Theatre, and *The Poems of Palladas of Alexandria* for Anvil Press.

JOHN HAYNES. Born 1937. Early childhood near Wolverhampton. Has taught in a school and in a College of Education at Leeds. At present teaching in the English department of a university in Nigeria.

JOHN HEATH-STUBBS. Born 1918 in London and educated at Oxford, where he was influenced by the teaching of C. S. Lewis and Charles Williams and by the friendship of Sidney Keyes, Drummond Allison and William Bell. Gregory Fellow in poetry at the University of Leeds 1952–5. Professor of English, University of Alexandria, 1955–8 and University of Michigan, Ann Arbor, 1960–61. At present lecturer in English Literature, College of St Mark and St John, Chelsea. Arts Council Award 1965. There are ten collections of verse, and, among the most recent, *Selected Poems* (1969). A selection of his poems is included in Penguin Modern Poets 20.

ZBIGNIEW HERBERT. Born 1924. One of the foremost poets of post-war Poland, where the phrase 'post-war' indicates survival through both the Nazi occupation and the subsequent political upheavals. He was over thirty when his first book of poems appeared. In his anthology *Post-War Polish Poetry* (1970) Milosz describes Herbert as the poet 'the most skilful in expressing . . . the collective experience of the last decades . . . can be called a poet of historical irony'. His *Selected Poems* (1968), translated by Czeslaw Milosz and Peter Dale Scott, are published in Penguin Modern European Poets.

NAZIM HIKMET. The foremost of modern Turkish poets. Was born in Salonika (then a Turkish province) in 1902. His first poems were produced in 1918. He became increasingly deeply involved in communism and visited Moscow in 1921. He returned to Turkey in 1924 and was imprisoned briefly for his political position in 1928. In 1938 he was again arrested for 'subversive political activities'; eleven years later a campaign was mounted for his release by intellectuals throughout the world. In 1950 he went on a hunger strike and was released the following year, whereupon he left for the Soviet Union. He died there in 1963. Taner Baybars, his English translator, has published *Selected Poems of Nazim Hikmet* (1967), *The Moscow Symphony* (1970), and *The Day Before Tomorrow* (1972).

GEOFFREY HILL. Born 1932 in Bromsgrove, Worcestershire. Educated at Bromsgrove High School and Keble College, Oxford, he is currently a lecturer in English at the University of Leeds. He has been awarded the Geoffrey Faber Memorial Prize and the Hawthornden Prize. There are three books of verse: *For the Unfallen* (1959), *King Log* (1968) and *Mercian Hymns* (1971). Hill's scrupulous work is complex yet frequently lyrical. A selection of his poems is in Penguin Modern Poets 8.

ANSELM HOLLO. Born 1934 in Helsinki and educated in Finland and Germany. Has travelled extensively and was a producer with the BBC European Service 1958–66. Since 1968 Visiting Lecturer in Poetry, University of Iowa. Has produced a lot of translations (see Haavikko and Saarikoski) and six collections of verse, the most recent of which is *Maya* (1970).

MIROSLAV HOLUB. Born 1923 in Pilsen. Attended School of Medicine, Charles University, Prague. Was a clinical pathologist 1953–4 and since then has done research on immunology in Prague and New York. Ian Milner and George Theiner have translated *Miroslav Holub: Selected Poems* (1967) for Penguin Modern European Poets, and Ian and Jarmila Milner translated *Although* (1971).

PETER HUCHEL. Born 1903 Berlin. Studied literature and philosophy in Berlin, Freiburg and Vienna. Awarded a poetry prize in 1932 for

Der Knabenteich but prevented its publication when the Nazis came to power. He was in the army from 1940 to 1945, when he returned from a Russian p.o.w. camp. Then worked as reader, director of drama and programmes director with East Berlin Radio. Chief editor of the literary journal *Sinn und Form* 1948–62; removed from the editorship. Left East Germany recently and is now living in Rome. Has published three volumes of poetry – *Gedichte* (1948), *Chausseen Chausseen* (1963), and *Die Sternenreise* (1967).

PHILIP LEVINE. Born 1928 in Detroit, Michigan, and educated at Wayne State University, Detroit. Now lives in Fresno, California. Has published five collections of verse: *On the Edge* (1963), *Not this Pig* (1968), *Five Detroits* (1970), *Red Dust* (1971), and *They Feed They Lion* (1972).

EMANUEL LITVINOFF. Born 1915 in the East End of London. Childhood and adolescence spent in the East End Jewish community. In the Pioneer Corps during the Second World War. Has published two volumes of poetry, now out of print, and two novels; has written several plays for television. An autobiographical sequence is due in 1972 and a novel, first of a trilogy, in 1973.

GEORGE MACBETH. Born Shotts, Scotland, 1932, and educated at Sheffield and Oxford, where he read classics. Widely travelled. Since 1965 a producer of programmes about literature for the BBC. Geoffrey Faber Memorial Prize, 1964. Has published eight collections of verse, of which the most recent is *Collected Poems* (1971). A selection of his poems is in Penguin Modern Poets 6.

SORLEY MACLEAN. Born 1911 on the island of Raasay. In the thirties he studied English literature under H. J. Grierson, but despite his concern with English poetry his first language is still Gaelic. By general consensus the foremost living Gaelic poet. Has been translated by Iain Crichton Smith, who writes in English and in Scots Gaelic. Maclean spent Second World War in Desert Army. Now headmaster of a school at Plockton, Wester Ross. Collection of his Gaelic poems published 1943. Most recent English publication is *Poems to Eimhir* (1971), translated by Crichton Smith. A selection of his more recent poetry (translated by himself) appears in *Four Points of a Saltire* (1970).

BARRY MACSWEENEY. Born 1948 in Newcastle. Editor of *The Blacksuede Boot*, a poetry magazine. Has published six books of verse, of which the most recent is *Brother Wolf* (Turret Press, 1972).

CHRISTOPHER MIDDLETON. Born 1926 in Truro, Cornwall. Formerly lecturer in German, King's College, London. Now Professor of Germanic Languages, University of Texas, Austin. Geoffrey Faber Memorial Prize, 1963. Has published three collections of verse, the two most recent being: *Our Flowers and Nice Bones* (1969) and *The Fossil Fish* (1970). Middleton, like Hamburger, is a distinguished translator of German poetry. See his *Georg Trakl: Selected Poems* (1968) and (with Hamburger) *Modern German Poetry (1910–60)* (1962).

EWART MILNE. Born 1903 in Dublin, educated Wicklow and Dublin. Has been a teacher, seaman, political student and farmer. Has published twelve books of poems; the last two are *A Garland for the Green* (1962) and *Time Stopped* (1967).

NORMAN NICHOLSON. Born in 1914 at Millom, Cumberland, and educated at local schools. The recipient of several awards, including the Cholmondeley Award for Poetry, 1967, and the Northern Arts Grant, 1969. Has published four verse plays and four books of poems – a fifth is on its way. The most recent book of verse is *A Local Habitation* (1972).

TOM PICKARD. Born Newcastle-on-Tyne 1946. With Connie Watson he founded the Morden Tower in 1963 and ran it for seven years. The Tower is notable not only for the variety of poets who have read there, but for its attraction of a regular audience. Pickard has published two collections of poetry, *High on the Walls* (1968), *The Order of Chance* (1971), and also a novel *Guttersnipe*.

MAILA PYLKKONEN. Born 1937. A poet and critic, who has published five books of poems.

MIKLÓS RADNÓTI. Born 1909, a Jewish Hungarian poet. Seven volumes of verse. His last, *Cloudy Sky*, written under extreme pressure, is his most famous. Served in forced labour camps from 1941 until he was shipped to the extermination camp at Bog, Yugoslavia. Killed in 1944. *Cloudy Sky*, translated by Polgar, Berg and Marks, appeared in 1971.

TOM RAWORTH. Born 1938 in London and, in the main, educated there. Studied Spanish at the University of Granada. Edited, printed and published *Outburst* magazine and Matrix Press Books, 1959–64. Founded the Goliard Press with Barry Hall. Resident Poet, University of Essex, 1969–70. Has published five books, most recently *Moving* (1971). A selection of his poems appears in Penguin Modern Poets 19.

TADEUSZ RÓŻEWICZ. Born in 1921 in Poland. One of Poland's foremost poets. Served in the guerrilla Home Army. His first poems, published immediately after the war, 'are short, nearly stenographic notes of horror, disgust, and derision at human values' (Milosz). Author of several plays which form part of the Polish theatre of the absurd. Adam Czerniawski has translated a selection of his poems – *Faces of Anxiety* (1969) – and is preparing a larger selection for Penguin Modern European Poets.

PENTTI SAARIKOSKI. Born 1927 in Finland. Poet, novelist and translator. *Selected Poems*, translated by Anselm Hollo, was published in 1967.

JON SILKIN. Born in London in 1930 and educated there, in Wales, and, after six years as a manual labourer, at the University of Leeds. Gregory Fellow in Poetry, University of Leeds, 1958–60. Geoffrey Faber Memorial Prize, 1966. Has taught in United States and was visiting lecturer, University of Iowa, 1968–9. Founded *Stand* 1952, and co-edited the magazine with Ken Smith and Catherine Lamb for six years. Has published five collections of poetry, the two most recent being *Poems New and Selected* (1966) and *Amana Grass* (1971). A critical book on the First World War poets, *Out of Battle*, published 1972. A selection of his poems is included in Penguin Modern Poets 7.

IAIN CRICHTON SMITH. Born 1928 on the Isle of Lewis, Outer Hebrides. His first language was Gaelic. Educated Aberdeen University. Since 1955 teacher of English, Oban High School, Argyllshire. Has published (in English) two novels and eight books of verse – the latest is *Selected Poems* (1971). Has translated from the Gaelic Sorley Maclean's *Poems to Eimhir* (1971), and has written poetry and fiction in Gaelic. Like Maclean is greatly concerned with the fate of the Gaelic language. A selection of his poems is included in Penguin Modern Poets 21.

KEN SMITH. Born 1938, Rudston, Yorks. Educated at Hull and the University of Leeds. Gregory Award, 1964. Tutor, Exeter College of Art, 1965–9. Currently teaching at Clark University and Holy Cross, Massachusetts. Co-editor of *Stand* for six years. Has published four collections of verse, the second of which was *The Pity* (1967), and the most recent *Work, Distances/Poems* (1971).

VLADIMIR SOLOUKHIN. Born 1924 into a peasant family at Alpino in the Soviet Union. Vladimir Technical School, then military service; entered Gorky Literary Institute, Moscow, in 1946. In his public utterances Soloukhin has, according to his translator, Daniel Weissbort, 'adhered to the Party Line and even attacked the younger poets in the *Literary Gazette*; but nevertheless he seems almost to regard the liberal–reactionary confrontation as irrelevant'.

WILLIAM STAFFORD. Born 1914 at Hutchinson, Kansas, and educated at the University of Kansas, Lawrence, and the University of Iowa. Active in pacifist organizations. Recipient of many prizes and awards, two of the more recent being National Book Award, 1963, and a Guggenheim Fellowship, 1966. Teaches English at Lewis and Clark College, Portland, Oregon. Has published seven books of verse including, recently, *The Rescued Year* (1966) and *Allegiances* (1970), and two volumes of criticism.

MARINA TSVETAYEVA. Born 1892. Her translator, Elaine Feinstein, considers her to be 'one of the greatest Russian poets of this century'. Spent most of her life in exile and neglect. When the Revolution came she was hostile, but remained in Moscow throughout the famine. One child died of malnutrition in 1920. Left the Soviet Union 1922 to join her husband in Prague, then lived in Prague, Berlin and Paris. In 1939 she followed her husband back to Russia after he had been exposed as a Russian agent, but he was killed on attempting to enter the country. She was unable to find work and when the war came was evacuated to Elabuga where, in 1941, she hanged herself. *Selected Poems*, translated by Elaine Feinstein, with the help of literal versions by Angela Livingstone, appeared in 1972 and will be reprinted in Penguin Modern European Poets.

GIUSEPPE UNGARETTI. Father from Lucca, but he himself was born at Alexandria in 1888. Went to Paris in 1912 and joined Apollinaire's circle. In the army (on the Isonzo front) during the First World War, as his poems attest: 'his war poems are a considerable part of his best early work' – Jonathan Griffin, one of his translators. Went to Brazil 1936 and taught for some years at Sao Paolo University. In 1942 became Professor of Contemporary Italian Literature in Rome, a post which he held until retirement. Has translated Shakespeare, Blake, Racine, Mallarmé and Góngora. *Vita di un uomo*, his collected poems, appeared in Italy in 1969 and he died the following year. A selection of his poems, the first to appear in the UK, has been published in Penguin Modern European Poets (1971), translated by Patrick Creagh.

CÉSAR VALLEJO. Born 1892 in the mountains of northern Peru. Worked in Lima and was imprisoned in Trujillo. Moved to Europe, where an intense concern with politics took precedence over his writing. His anger at the suffering caused by capitalism in the Depression led to some of his finest writing. Wrote poems against the Spanish Civil War but died in France in 1938, before it ended.

ANDREI VOZNESENSKY. Born 1933 in Moscow. Part of his early childhood was spent in the ancient city of Vladimir. 1941–4 lived with his mother in Kurgan, the Urals. Studied architecture at the Moscow Architectural Institute for a while. Like Yevtushenko, Voznesensky is an extremely popular poet in the Soviet Union. A selection of his poems, *Antiworlds*, appeared in translation in 1967.

JEFFREY WAINWRIGHT. Born 1944 in Stoke-on-Trent, took a degree at the University of Leeds. Has published one collection of poems: *The Important Man* (1970).

TED WALKER. Born 1934, Lancing, Sussex, and read modern languages at Cambridge. Gregory Award, 1964. Cholmondeley Award for Poetry, 1966. Has travelled widely in Europe and has been a full-time writer since 1967. Four collections of verse, the second of which was *Fox on a Barn Door* (1965) and the most recent *The Night Bathers* (1970).

NATHAN WHITING. Born 1946. Supplies no biography. Has published *While Courting the Sergeant's Daughter* (1969).

JAMES WRIGHT. Born 1927 at Martin's Ferry, Ohio. Educated Kenyon College and University of Washington, Seattle. Studied with

Crowe Ransom and Theodore Roethke. Fulbright Scholarship (Vienna) 1952–3. Other grants, including the Guggenheim. Now lives in New York City. Informally associated with Robert Bly and the Sixties Press. Has translated, among others, Trakl, Vallejo and Neruda. Four books of verse, latterly *The Branch Will Not Break* (1963) and *Shall We Gather at the River* (1968).

YEVGENY YEVTUSHENKO. Born 1933, and, with Voznesensky, among the most popular of the younger Soviet poets. Probably the most widely translated of the post-war generation in Russia. A revised and enlarged edition of Yevtushenko's poems, selected and translated by George Reavey, was published under the title of *The Poetry of Yevgeny Yevtushenko* in 1969. A selection of his poems has been published in Penguin Modern European Poets (1962), translated by Robin Milner-Gulland and Peter Levi, S.J.

NATAN ZACH. Born 1930 in Berlin of an Italian mother and a German father. Went to Israel in 1935 and lived in Haifa until 1946. Studied philosophy at the Hebrew University, Jerusalem. Has published four books of poems, one critical work and a volume of poems translated from the Arabic. Now a lecturer in Hebrew literature at the University of Tel-Aviv. A selection of his poems, translated by Jon Silkin together with the poet, was published under the title of *Against Parting* (1967).

INDEX OF TITLES AND FIRST LINES

In cases where the title and the first line are identical only the title is given. Titles are in italics. Where the title forms only part of the first line it is italicized and the rest of the line is given normally.

INDEX OF POETS

MORE ABOUT PENGUINS

Penguinews, which appears every month, contains details of all the new books issued by Penguins as they are published. From time to time it is supplemented by *Penguins in Print*, which is a complete list of all available books published by Penguins. (There are well over four thousand of these.)

A specimen copy of *Penguinews* will be sent to you free on request, and you can become a subscriber for the price of the postage. For a year's issues (including the complete lists) please send 30p if you live in the United Kingdom, or 60p if you live elsewhere. Just write to Dept EP, Penguin Books Ltd, Harmondsworth, Middlesex, enclosing a cheque or postal order, and your name will be added to the mailing list.

Note: *Penguinews* and *Penguins in Print* are not available in the U.S.A. or Canada